Andy & Patty

Enjoy

STELLA

Andy & Ruth

Junior

STELLA

The Story She Buried Along

With Her Parents.

Thomas Fahey

This is a work of non-fiction. Names, places, characters, dates, and Incidents are all factual. Much of the dialogue is imaginative based on what little personal information is known of the characters.

"STELLA" copyright 2020 by Thomas Fahey

Published by Thomas Fahey

ISBN 978-1-71612-457-0

FIRST EDITION

For my wife Kathy and my friends Tom,
Denny, and Harry

They each played a part in editing my work,
pushing me to write, and buoying my spirit
through the years of research and writing.
Thank you.

"Stella"

Table of Contents

Introduction

Late December, 1929, five a.m. on a still, dark, damp road. A sheriff spots a suspect not far from the scene of a crime. Stopping his car to question the man on the road, the sheriff's buttonless coat blows open revealing his gold badge. Fearful, the stranger draws his gun and fires two shots. Falling wounded, the sheriff discharges six shots from his weapon. The lawman lies bleeding on the road.

This scene looks like a film noir 'whodunit.' Instead, it introduces the real-life story of the sheriff, his wife, and their young daughter. That girl is my Mother, Stella Mae Lange Fahey. The sheriff is her Father, Herman Thomas Lange. The sheriff's wife, Stella's Mother, is Mayme Lange. As it flows down its heart-rending path, the tale is locked deep within Stella's heart. It is never shared.

The blank pages of the story of Herman and Mayme and Stella open to me a quarter of a century later among the tombstones that fill the Greendale Indiana Cemetery. I begin my wondering and discovery with the following trip.

~

I am six years old. It's 1953. It is September, but the day is delivered on a coattail of summer. I slouch, feet twitching on the scratchy seat of Dad's bulky black Ford sedan. Mom and Dad sit quietly in the front seat as we drive from Cincinnati to Aurora, Indiana to visit Grandma and Grandpa Fahey. We celebrate Grandma's birthday. My neck tightens as I think about the trip, but my smile widens as I think about our destination.

"Are we there yet?"

1

I recognize familiar landmarks along the way. My stomach churns as the thick, oily stench of the Gulf refinery along Route 128 burns inside my throat. The heavy, acrid gas smell assails my nose but tells me we are nearer our destination. I scoot up in my seat and look out at the dirty grey, rusted tanks holding the noxious liquid.

"I'm feeling sick. Are we there yet?"

We are further down the road. I see the old junk yard on Route 50 and know we are close. I wonder how all these old dusty, dented wrecks arrive at this endless field of corroded fenders and rotting tires. My mind wanders the endless expanse of road, as I stretch my legs and kick my feet at the back of the front seat.

"Are we there yet?"

Out the window I see fields high with green waves of summer corn on each side of Route 50. I know this sight. The light yellow scent of grain tickles my nose. We are close. We turn off the highway. We wind up a steep hill. This isn't the way to Grandma's. I slump back again in my seat.

"What's this? We're not there."

We turn off the road steering between two large columns of stacked, chiseled rocks. Massive black, wrought-iron gates hang from these totems. We tunnel through rows of towering, dark-trunked evergreens. At the end of the tree-lined path, we roll past a sea of stark white stones poking up row by row through green waves of grass. Small flags of red, white, and blue-hued fabric wave over each stone like a field rich with radiant wildflowers—bright red poppies and soft blue morning glories.

"I know we're not there."

The car stops. My lip curls. Angry tears leak from the

corners of my eyes. Mom and Dad slide out of the car. Mom opens my door. I don't want to get out.

"Where are we? We're not there."

We cross the road and stop at a large double polished limestone rock etched with flowers, swirls, and some words.

"Where are we?"

Mom grabs my hand. "This is Grandpa and Grandma Lange's tombstone."

I stop, my feet digging at the grass. "Who are they?"

Mom tries to explain, "A tombstone helps us recall loved ones no longer with us." Placing some flowers near the tombstone, Mom turns to me, "We come here to remember your grandparents."

Who are these people beneath the limestone rock—a rock inscribed with birth dates and death dates? Herman Thomas Lange was born in 1889 and died in 1929. Mayme Gesell Lange was born in 1886 and died in 1944. On every tombstone are a birth date, a dash, and a death date. On that dash between birth and death lives are lived. On that dash people live meaningful or meaningless lives. On that dash between birth and death Herman and Mayme lived their lives. What does the chiseled dash on Herman and Mayme's tombstone reveal for me?

Lange Tombstone Greendale Cemetery

~

Stella is unable to recount the tale of the couple buried in Greendale. Lacking counseling or support, Mom locks all of her parents' history away along with the grief, the longing, the loss.

Stella kept a diary beginning in 1935, a full five years after the traumatic loss of her father. She wished for a better year. She wished her mother would not be so sad. She wished her job at the distillery was steady. Her disposition was gloomy and somewhat despondent as noted by this February 5, 1935 excerpt. "Dear Diary: Same old thing. Nothing ever happens. Stayed home tonight. Guess I'll never have any more luck. My good times seem to be gone. Help me."

Stella's Diary 1934…1936

After the death of her father Stella seems to be lost and alone. I wish that she had journalized her experiences at the time of Herman's death and the years of Mayme's struggles to hold the family together. Stella's words on the pages of a diary could have blunted her pain. Lacking a journal by Stella, I begin each chapter by fictionalizing what she might have thought and felt.

I realize the story is forever lost when I visit Mom on my 48th birthday. On this special day for both of us she does not even know me. Her stories are gone. Alzheimer's locks the story of my Lange Grandparents. It is now that I determine to unlock the book of my Grandparents' lives.

I carve out time from my weekly visits with Mom so that I can research microfilmed local newspapers, census records, county histories, and local plat and property records at the Aurora and Lawrenceburg Libraries. Genealogist Joyce Baer of the Lawrenceburg Public Library helps with all things southeastern Indiana. *The Lawrenceburg Press, The Lawrenceburg Register* and *The Aurora Press* offer narratives of the shooting of Herman Lange, the appointment of Mayme to complete his unexpired term as sheriff, and the capture, trial and conviction of his murderer, James Anderson.

The newspaper articles are static. They are two dimensional and flat. They are little more than ink that has soaked into a thirsty page. The pages have a story, but the story has no life. Mom should be the artist to breathe life onto the canvas that is her story of Herman and Mayme. I will need much more than the microfilm articles of the local newspapers to complete the portrait of Herman and Mayme.

My Wife did ask Stella to paint a portrait of her childhood on the Family's Wrights' Corner farm. Mom's recount of Lange family life enlivens five pages of pale blue stationery in Kathy's hand. The family's early farm years are drawn from bright, flowing, cheery memories. Memory of

Herman's death, his killer's trial, and the long wait for justice is written in short, static statements of fact. The family story changes from light and loving to dark and mournful like the flip of an electric switch.

To expand this portrait I research details of agricultural life in southeastern Indiana in the 1920's. Daniel Nelson and Mary Neth's books speak of everyday small farm life in early twentieth century Indiana. Dearborn County Recorder, Glenn Wright helps me along the way. He offers insight into the location of the Lange's family farm.

I search for the Lange's story in the history of southeastern Indiana. Agriculture, Depression, Politics and Ku Klux Klan all paint the landscape which was southern Indiana of the 1920's. Dennis Nordin, Roy Scott, William Wilson, and James H. Madison detail changes in Indiana farming that provide a backdrop for Herman's move of his family from the small rural farm to an urban life in the courtroom and jail house. Edward Behr and Marc McCutcheon detail the evils of Prohibition that plague the country during Herman's term as sheriff. Research transforms my portrait of Herman and Mayme and Stella from a faded dull sepia tone to a brighter, vibrant color.

Arthur Wenzel, historian and Deputy County Surveyor, digs through old newspapers stored in the basement of the County Administration Building. His findings document history needed to add Herman's name to the National Law Enforcement Officers Memorial in Washington D. C.

Sheriff David Lusby of Dearborn County opens my mind to the sheriff's life in the times—low pay, lack of equipment, and evil everywhere. Dedication to the job and the people of the county drives a lawman. Dave's passion drives me to find the elusive and mysterious 'why' for the clemency, parole and pardon of Herman's murderer, James Anderson.

Dave helps me piece together the news stories of the incidents at the Whitewater "bootleg camps" and the shooting near Longenecker's Station. Dave walks me through the steps that Herman Lange and James Anderson would have taken on that December morning. The walk with Dave put me in Herman's shoes.

As Sheriff of Dearborn County in 2010, Dave tackles the obstacles needed to add Herman Lange's name to the engraved walls of the National Law Enforcement Memorial in Washington, D. C. In the fall of 2010 Dave helps etch Herman's name onto the Indiana Police Memorial. Here Mayme is also recognized. Mayme is the first woman sheriff in the State of Indiana.

Throughout the Lange story, people intersect the lives of Herman and Mayme. Folks, such as Dearborn County Circuit Court Judge Charles A. Lowe and Cincinnati Cal Crim Detective Ora M. Slater, come to life on the pages of the many local newspapers and even the works of historians Eugene B. Block and Thomas Crowl.

The records of the Dearborn County Circuit Court Case No. 3603 and the Franklin County Circuit Court Case No. 2018 provide an ongoing narrative of The *State of Indiana vs. James Anderson.* This view of the murder trial of Herman Lange's murderer follows from the Grand Jury Indictment all the way through the trial, conviction, sentencing, request for retrial, and appeal of the sentence to the Indiana Supreme Court. Governors Paul McNutt's *Executive Order #8266,* Henry Schricker's Executive *Order # 17970,* and Harold Hanley's *Executive Order # 22180* show the killer's sentence commutation, parole, and final pardon through the years 1933 to 1960.

No resources uncover the anguish, frustration, fear, and mourning Mayme and Stella feel for years after Herman's death. I watched Mom shut out all memories of the loss of her father. I witnessed the traumatic seizures unleashed by her pained remembrance of the past and fear of the future.

The story of Herman and Mayme slowly opens its pages to me. It begins at the carved tombstone in Greendale Cemetery beneath which lie my grandparents. As the story meanders through my mind, it reveals it's meaning at another set of carved stones—the stone monuments at the Indiana Law Enforcement and Fire Fighters Memorial in Indianapolis and at the National Law Enforcement Officers Memorial in Washington, D.C. These stones reveal everything, standing as tribute to the life and sacrifice of Sheriff Herman Lange, and as such they likewise honor Mayme.

I begin my journey. I turn everything over to the main character Stella Mae Lange Fahey—Herman and Mayme's Daughter, my Mother. To bring all the research together in a lifelike voice, I write the narrative in my Mom's voice. I put myself in her shoes.

Now Stella begins her story.

1

"In the Beginning"

Mom and Dad have been married for twelve years. That seems like a long time to me.

Stella Mae Lange – My Journal, 11/29/1923

My name is Stella Mae Lange. Please call me Stella. I suppose I should tell my story beginning with Mom and Dad and their parents. It doesn't seem right to talk about myself until I've laid out how I got to this point. I know nothing but life on our farm. I see enough of all the relatives to be able to lay out a pretty good picture of what Mom calls our 'Family Tree.'

Grandma Anna Marie and Grandpa John Gesell,—Mom's parents—lived on a farm in Highland Township in Franklin County near the Trinity Lutheran Church. Their flat parcel of land lay along gravel covered Highland Center Road. I recall horses and a big field of corn and wheat on their farm.

My great-grandparents Johan and Caroline Bossert Gesell's farm lay not far from there at Klemmes Corner. They were good, front-pew Lutherans. They donated a parcel of land upon which a new Lutheran Church and cemetery was built.

Trinity Lutheran
Church, Klemme's
Corner, Indiana

Johan Gesell's Trinity Lutheran Church

Mary Magdalena, or Mayme, my Mom was born on September 9, 1886. She grew up on that Highland Township farm with three brothers and two sisters. Betty was her favorite sibling. Before Mayme finished the eighth grade, she buried her Mother. After Grandma died, Mom yoked her broad shoulders with the care for her widowed father. She grew up fast and hard. I never heard Mom wince or complain about the challenge to keep their farm afloat. Mom loved that farm and did all she could to keep it going. She carried a fondness for the horses and led them furrowing the pastures each spring. She helped Grandpa John keep his feet firm in the rich farm dirt, hiring herself as a housekeeper for a private family in the area. Mom tackled every undertaking with strength and determination.

Dad's parents, William and Louisia Lange, were farmers. The rolling, rocky terrain of York Township in Dearborn County, Indiana was home for them. The ground was tough plowing, but the breezes blowing across the tops of the hills from Wrights Corner invited the bees to pollinate all the fruit trees and grape vines on the Lange's farm.

Dad, Herman Thomas Lange, was born on September 3, 1889. His older brother was the son of Christina, Grandpa William's first wife, who died in 1883. Herman's Mom Louisa had five sons and three daughters. My Grandma and Grandpa Lange moved the family to a farm in Manchester Township where Dad then went to school. He finished the eighth grade there and spent his teen-age and young adult years working the Lange farm along with his brothers.

Reverend Christian Busse's St. Stephens Lutheran Church

11

The Lange's also carried strong ties to the Lutheran Church. Dad's great-uncle, Reverend Christian Busse was pastor at St. Stephen's Lutheran Church in Manchester Township. He preached there more than 28 years. William and Louisa were buried in the church's cemetery.

Herman and Mayme Wedding November 29, 1911

Mom told me the story of meeting Dad at a church social in Klemmes Corner. It was a pretty good carriage ride from Manchester to Highland Township, but Dad seemed to find a way to stoke the fires of his new-found friendship with Mom on a regular basis. Chores filled their week, but Sunday held the promise of a little hand-holding after church.

Mom and Dad wed in 1911. Aunt Betty Gesell, Mom's sister, and Uncle Bill Lange, Dad's brother, witnessed the couple's marriage at Trinity Lutheran Church on November 29.

They spent their early wedded life in Greendale on Kansas Street. In the family's early years Dad worked for the Big Four Railroad—the Cleveland, Cincinnati, Chicago, and St. Louis Railway. The railway's tracks, yards and stations dotted the Dearborn and Franklin County area of southern Indiana. Dad told me his job was policing the rail yards looking for vagrants, hobos, and train-hoppers. It sounded exciting to me, but Dad always said it was a terrible way to make a living. Raised on a farm, he wished to return to a farm.

Now you're caught up. I've told you where we came from. Now let me begin our tale. Join me in my story with my Dad Herman and my Mom Mayme.

2

"The Early Years"

The December snow covers our farm in a cold, white blanket.
The cold is chased when Dad hitches our horse to the sled and
rides us around the neighborhood to the tune of sleigh bells.
                    Stella Mae Lange – *My Journal, 12/20/1923*

I was born in Greendale, Indiana on July 6, 1914. A few
months later Mom (Mayme) and Dad (Herman) purchased
seventy-one acres in Wrights Corner. I am ever so glad they
got the farm. It's fragrance fills my childhood days.

Our little frame and stucco house stands close to the
road. The barn sits back from the house—down the road by the
dirt path that bounds the sunset side of the farm. It houses our
horses, a few cows and all their hay. A small shed holds Dad's
tools, plow, and carriage harness.

A windmill rises up behind the barn. It supplies the milk
house with cold water. I carry water one bucket at a time from
the well to the trough by the barn. It's hard work but the horses
appreciate my efforts.

Mom works the small vegetable garden behind the barn.
Dad digs it up and Mom plants it each spring. This is her pride
and joy. She keeps us fed with fresh cabbage, beans, tomatoes,
carrots, whatever the season offers. She cans a lot each fall.

Every autumn the fruit cellar shelves fill with jars of fruits, vegetables, pickles, relishes, jams and jellies. Mom stores potatoes, apples, onions, winter squash, butternut squash and pumpkins in the cool cellar as well. Dad heads to the Aurora Roller Mill to have much of his wheat harvest ground into flour. We travel to town for salt, lard, meal and little else. I don't remember ever being hungry.

Herman on Farm in Beekeeper Gear

Near the east side of the house stands an orchard. Fruit trees line the area. Summer ends with a peachy, juice-dripping

15

sweetness rivering down my chin. The crisp tart taste of apple crunches across my teeth in fall. Rows of grape vines run parallel toward the back of the orchard. Walking barefoot—ripe black peels squishing between my toes—my nose flares with the almost yeast-like tang of the late summer berries. I steer clear of the orchard as much as I can as Dad has several hives dotting the front of the fruit trees. I don't like bees. Dad dons his beekeeper outfit and mask and smokes the hive and harvests their honey.

Mom warns me to steer clear of the smoked hives. She says my creamy skin is mighty tempting for any of the bees fleeing the masked beekeeper. I was stung once, but Mom whipped up a poultice of baking soda and water to keep the swelling and burning and itching down. Even with all that, my arm bumped up into a fire red patch.

Mom tends a small flower garden near the orchard. Bright red hyacinths and yellow cockscombs and pink hollyhocks and white snapdragons and purple crocus render the pollen the bees crave. We reap the rewards. Mom uses the honey in place of sugar to bake. Fresh apples and fresh honey meld into one fine apple pie. I stand aside Mom as she shows me how to flour the rolling pin, press out the fresh dough, press the golden crust into the pie plate, and gently crimp the edges in a dainty, fluted edge. My nose gathers the tart, just-baked streams rising up through the flakey-latticed pie. I love that.

My step lightens, my eyes brighten, my smile widens in fall. Apples hang ready to be picked. I can't reach high enough to get all of them, but I borrow one of Mom's clothes-props and I shake loose most of the fresh crop. We pack all the good apples in bushels and pecks. Dad blends the rest into some tasty, tangy cider. He even bottles a few gallons of vinegar. The real fun comes on the weekend. With a few days off school, I sit out front along Route 48 and wave at cars passing by from Lawrenceburg and Aurora and even Cincinnati. They stop and I sell them the bounty of Dad's harvest.

Stella on Farm with Apples

We have cows. Mom milks, Dad pitches the hay into their pen. My chin tightens and my back stiffens when it's time to separate the cream from the milk. I pour the fresh milk into the separator. I turn the handle to spin the container and force the lighter skim milk from the cream. There's a bell on this contraption that rings if I don't turn the handle fast enough to spin the bowl to separate the cream from the milk. As hard as I try, that bell always rings. No amount of foot stomping eases my jitters. We use a lot of the milk ourselves, the thick, smooth, buttery cream being my favorite. I can taste a little sweet-cream drizzled on slices of Dad's fresh-picked peaches. Weekly trips down the road with Dad to sell cream at the Kyle Creamery delight me.

Kyle Creamery State Route 48

Chickens populate the farm yard. After school I gather eggs from the nests hoping the hens won't peck at my fingers. The family sells eggs on the road in front of the house. Dad catches and kills Sunday chicken dinner for Mom to cook. The nasty job of cleaning all the feathers from the fresh killed chicken often falls to me. I wince and my brow furrows, but the feathers come off no quicker unless I give the bird a little hot water bath first. A clothes pin for my nose and Mom's old high-topped leather boots dress me for cleaning the chicken coop.

In spring Mom picks dandelion leaves and makes them into a delicious salad. She serves the dandelion leaves wilted, with hot vinegar and sugar and water and bacon drippings poured over them. Dad brews a rich tea from the roots of a sassafras sapling. We dig, clean, and boil the roots brewing a dark reddish colored tea. It cures whatever ails you. It also tastes good.

"Mayme on Tony the Wonder Horse"

We have horses. I named them 'Tony the Wonder Horse' like Tom Mix's wonderful horse and 'Blackie' for the big black one. Dad uses the horses to plow and harvest. In the spring, Dad burns the corn stalks left from the previous year's crop and spreads manure on the fields as fertilizer. He hooks the plow to the backs of Tony and Blackie and follows behind

19

digging furrows into the hard ground. If he runs into a stubborn tree stump, he hitches a chain to their backside and urges them to pull the old tree right up and out.

In winter Dad harnesses Tony and hitches the sleigh to his back. The harness bells ching, ching, chings a tinkling winter melody as the horse whisks the sleigh through the snow. I pray for snow just so Dad will get the sleigh out and drive us around. We shush down the street and pick up my friends. With a little snow and the horse pulling the carriage down the lane, we break out in a chorus of "Jingle Bells."

Farm life is not easy. In the busy season from spring until fall, the family makes few trips to town. Days begin early. The family rises before daylight every morning. Get the horses in to feed and get them ready for the field. Milk the cows. Finally, eat breakfast, a large meal for a long, hard day ahead. With the sun barely peeking over the horizon Dad harnesses the horses and heads to the fields. Gather eggs, separate cream, churn butter, feed the chickens, plant and harvest, clean the chicken house, clean the outhouse, wash the clothes, can and jar fruits and vegetables. Start all over again.

We have no electricity, no indoor plumbing. Farming for Mom and Dad is hard work, with long days and little money. They cheer in caring for their stock, working the soil, and watching the crops grow. They raise most of their own food. They enjoy a life more independent than that of city folk. I never see them without a smile on their face and pleasure in their voice.

I walk a half mile to Wrights Corner Elementary each day. My memory of life on the family farm overflows with fond recollections. The simple life culled from the harvest of hard work feeds my loving remembrance of our farm days.

Fragrant farm memories fill my childhood days. I love our life on the farm.

Stella on the Farm

~

Drive down the same stretch of road in Wrights Corner today and you would see farms just like the Lange's farm of the 1920's. The farm house no longer sits on the spot where the Lange's farmed for years. Not far from where they lived there is still a family farm today. On Indiana 48 is the Busse Family farm. Busses are descended of Reverend Christian Busse founder of the Manchester Lutheran Church. Fred Lange and

Hannah Busse Lange were Herman's Grandparents. The Lange's farm of seventy-one acres sits almost directly across Indiana 48 from the Busse's farm of today. In the fall you can buy cider and apples and pumpkins at the Busse's roadside stand just as you could in the 1920's at Lange's seventy-one acre farm.

Busse's Farm Across from Lange's Seventy-one Acres

It would seem that the Lange's rural southern Indiana farm provided abundant blessings for the young family. Everything this young family needed seemed to grow from their seventy-one acres. They have carved out a good life for themselves.

3

"How Ya Gonna Keep 'em Down on the Farm?"[1]

Dad keeps looking at the new tractor at the farm down the road. He says we can't afford one. Mom says we'll do fine without one. Me, I like our horses and hope we never get a Fordson.

Stella Mae Lange – *My Journal, 04/15/1924*

Mom and Dad never discuss money and certainly never hint of struggles to keep the farm. Entering the fourth grade, I notice subtle changes in our happy, comfortable farm life. Riding to town or church on Sunday, I see small wooden "For Sale" signs peppering the side of the highway. Mom and Dad talk in whispered tones about the signs as we drive by them.

At Sunday services we see fewer families flumped in the pews. Fewer friendly faces show up at Kyle's Creamery. Leo Fahey at Aurora's Kroger store balks at the offer to run a tab

[1] Young and Sam M. Lewis, Waterson, Berlin & Snyder Co in New York,

191

on groceries. Hard candy requires a penny, not a promise of payment next week. Fewer familiar faces from up 'around the horn' frequent the Aurora Feed Store.

"Dad, where are all the people going?"

He grumbles, "Many just can't afford to stay on their farms anymore. They are leaving to find jobs and to live in the city."

Mom whispers, "We're fine, Stella."

I believe her, but we limit our trips to town more and more. Movies still render a great escape, but we now go to Lawrenceburg's Walnut Theatre maybe once a month. I can remember when we enjoyed a new flick every week.

One thing doesn't change. In late summer and early fall, a great flurry of activity overtakes all the area farms. When Dad's wheat grows golden-harvest ready, he contacts one of the neighbors who has a threshing machine. The massive, mechanical thresher and about a dozen neighboring men turn out to help cut, bale, and stack the summer's wheat. I and a couple of the girls who tag along run water out to the men as they work. I always have a grand old time with my school chums. Mom prepares a large noon meal for the crew. Day by day I see the group and the thresher move from farm to farm helping with the harvest.

Before winter sets in, this same group activity moves along Route 48—men filling and patching holes in the graveled road. In snow their harnessed horses drag the road free of the deep white stuff. If the neighbors don't take care of the highway, it becomes difficult to maneuver or even impassable.

Dad says, "The road acts as lifeline to the city. We all must maintain it for the common good."

I hear talk of a lot of new powered equipment availing

itself to farmers. Dad has a big old 1917 half-ton Ford Model T Road Truck. It gets us back and forth to town and church. Sometimes it helps Dad drag a tough tree trunk out of his way. It looks to me like a good tractor might help with all the chores on the farm. The Engelking family across the road has one. It looks like it does fine for them.

Dad says, "I won't spend money on mechanization as long as we have good helpful neighbors"

He looks hard at the Fordson tractor down at the Ford Dealer in Lawrenceburg. His eyes light up at the sight of its powerful engine and huge wedge-treaded wheels. I am glad when I overhear him tell Mom he doesn't have the $625 to get that tractor.

I chuckle, "No machine will replace 'Tony the Wonder Horse.'"

Arms outstretched and folded over bent knees, I sit up in bed some nights and strain my ears to hear Mom and Dad's muffled conversations at the kitchen table.

Dad assures, "I can still make the farm work without a tractor or a thresher."

Worried, Mom says, "We can't stay afloat with the prices falling on everything we grow."

Dad chokes back a rough mumble, "We invest nickels and only get pennies back."

Mom firms her voice and I can imagine her peering over the top of her spectacles saying, "Herman, the price on a bag of flour just went up another nickel. Corn seeds are up twenty cents. Still, we're lucky to get seventy cents for a bushel of corn today. We used to get a dollar. It doesn't add up. More money goes out than comes in."

Herman argues, "We can make it."

I hear the question rise from Mom's throat, "How can we continue?"

Next morning at breakfast, the smiles return to their faces. Their eyes assure me everything will be fine. The good times are short-lived.

On a chilled early spring morning when Dad should be leading Tony and Blackie to dig up the fields, I see him lead the big black horse out of the barn and tie him to the back of the old Ford truck.

I run out, grab Dad by his coat sleeve, and yell, "What are you doing with Blackie?"

"I'm taking him down the road. Gonna' sell him to my brother, Alpha."

Dad always speaks straight forward. He looks you straight in the eye when he talks. This time is different. He buries his eyes in the red mud at his feet and says, "We're a little behind on some bills. I'm going to Alpha as he'ill give me enough for Blackie to get us through this crunch."

I choke back a sob

"We'll be fine. We just need to work at things a little harder. If things improve, we may get Blackie back."

Dad never talks much. Mom talks, Dad works. That night after supper he coughs in his forearm, swallows a deep breath, and struggles to lay out our troubles. He doesn't stop even when the dishes are put away. He sits down and continues to tell us his hopes for the future. They are hopes not dreams that he talks about. He knows things have to change. He knows that hard work will get us through. He also knows that we must drag our heads out of the clouds and dig our feet into the dark, Indiana clay. I don't understand all Dad's words, but I listen and try to absorb them. I am concerned about what we will do without Blackie. Dad concerns himself with our survival tomorrow, next week and next year.

"Back in 1914 when we bought this place, farm land was still relatively cheap. The war pushed demand and prices up a bunch. We were in good shape."

Mom, always the family penny-pincher, says, "We had no problem making the mortgage in our early years."

"Yeh, things were too good. Many farmers added more acreage to their farms. People saw the dollar signs and got greedy. They borrowed, got more acres, and prayed for a windfall."

"I don't understand, Dad. What's all this got to do with losing Blackie?"

Dad counters, "Well, in 1920 the government ended its guarantees. Farm prices dropped back naturally. Farmers continued to produce more than demanded; the price of goods sold fell by half."

I'm determined to win this conversation, pleading, "Can't we just grow more?"

"We can't plow our way out of trouble. These prices have remained low while the cost of goods and services farmers had to buy increased. People who had borrowed money could not repay their loans."

Mom, ever the bookkeeper adds, "We can count our blessings. We never over borrowed even when the plat next door became available."

"You're right, still neighbors selling their farms got less than what they owed. Low prices and high expenses set a depressing tone for us farmers."

"Dad and I have tried to keep a tight lid on the cookie jar."

27

"Foreclosures loom like a dark cloud for our friends. If we were to sell our seventy-one acres in Wrights Corner, we would find ourselves under water—drowning in debt, owing more on our mortgage than we could sell for."

Mom takes her glasses off and asks, "How can we keep our farm, Herman?"

"I've been looking into a fix for our crunch."

I shout, "You gonna buy a tractor?"

"Not hardly. I have a friend who will buy our farm and hold the deed. Dearborn Circuit Court Judge Charles A. Lowe offered me a job as his riding bailiff."

"When were you planning on telling me about this, Herman?"

"Give me time. It all fell together so quick. I didn't have a chance to tell you about it."

"So, what's the big plan?"

"Remember, I met the judge back when I worked for the Big Four Railroad. I used to bring hoboes into court before him. He always liked the work I did. The manager down at the Aurora State Bank told him I was behind on the mortgage. The judge put his head into figuring how to help us and made me an offer."

"And what is this offer?"

"The judge picks up the mortgage. I can still work the farm. I can repay the judge over time with the money I make as bailiff."

I think Mom hears everything Dad says. She is not happy that he might go to work at the courthouse. She knows this means he will carry a gun again. Her eyes—now a deeper, darker shade of brown—betray her emotions. She hopes for a better outcome.

Me, all I heard was we'll keep the farm. Tony and the cows and the chickens will stay, too. My grin belies my pleasure.

~

Scenes like this, unfolding with the Lange's, were the main course served across kitchen tables throughout Indiana farmland in the 1920's. Like gnawing on an overcooked chuck roast, farmers chewed on the tough, gristly facts of agricultural depression. The meat of the conversations was hard to swallow. Many choked on the inability to digest the events troubling their agricultural livelihood.

Indiana farmers started down the road to depression in the early 1920s. Even before World War I, Woodrow Wilson encouraged farmers to overplant and feed the world. The government guaranteed farmers high prices for their crops. Farmers cultivated more acres. They borrowed money to buy more land and machinery. Demand for farm land increased and so did its value. From 1914 when the Lange's purchased their farm to 1919 the price of crops doubled.

In the early 1920's, small farm owners in southeastern Indiana like the Lange's struggled to maintain their existence. By the late 1920's the total number of Indiana farms declined by over half. The number of farms decreased, but the average size of farms increased from 103 acres to 193 acres. There were fewer farms but the larger farms that survived produced more and varied crops and livestock. Changes in farming in the 1920's reshaped Herman, Mayme, and Stella's lives.

Some details made it easy for small farmers such as the Lange's to hang onto their agrarian life for a while. Daniel

Nelson suggested that small farm "success depended more on labor than capital. Many prosperous Midwestern farmers cut hay with a scythe, planted corn by hand, spread manure by pitchfork, and grew their own seeds. Their achievements were the results of good organization and management, especially the management of their time and energies."[2]

"Fundamental change in agriculture came partly from the application of technology to farming…the twentieth century brought rapid change. Most important was the tractor, which best symbolized modern agriculture. The percentage of farms with tractors increased from 4 percent in 1920 to 22 percent in 1930." [3] Based on census results, there were 9,230 tractors on 203,126 farms in 1920. This number grew in 1930 to 41,979 tractors.

"The Fordson, introduced 1917, was the first inexpensive tractor. Though it could do little more than pull a plow and was unsafe, it underlined the potential of farm mechanization in the automobile era. In the following decade manufacturers introduced major improvements … power take off…enabled the tractor engine to power implements, the all-purpose tractor, designed to cultivate row crops; the power lift,…simplified turning; and the pneumatic tire."[4] Like many small farmers, the Langes could not afford a tractor. Modernization with tractors made it possible for farmers to turnover acres that had been used for horse feed to other cash crops.[5]

---

[2] Daniel Nelson, *Farm and Factory, Workers in the Midwest 1880-1990* (Indiana University Press, 1995), 70

[3] William E. Wilson, *Indiana: A History* (Indiana University Press, 1966), 263

[4] Daniel Nelson, *Farm and Factory, Workers in the Midwest 1880-1990* (Indiana University Press, 1995), 70

[5] James H. Madison, *Indiana Through Tradition and Change, A History of the Hoosier State and Its People, 1920-1945*(Indiana Historical Society ,

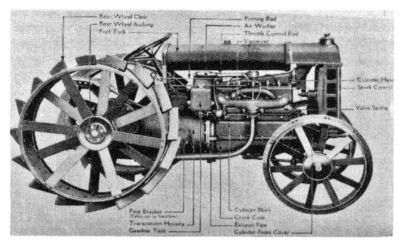

1917 Fordson [6]

Despite the great changes in agriculture, many farmers resisted the modern in place of traditional. Many continued traditional ways because they could not afford the new machinery. Getting by was their immediate need. It was difficult to look past the immediate to the long range promised future returns of mechanization.

Quite often small farms could not gain the economies of scale that modern machinery brought to large farms. Even if a small farmer could afford a tractor, he may not gain from its use. He would need to buy more land to enjoy the benefits of modernization. Modernize and grow could be costly propositions for small farmers "For many families who owned middle-sized farms"(between 50 and 175 acres)"the necessary response was either to attempt to buy more land and increase the farm size or to move to town or city to jobs in an auto parts factory, a knitting mill, or a grocery store."[7]

1982), 153-155
[6] R.B Gray, *The Agricultural Tractor, 1855-1950*, (American Society of Agricultural Engineers, 1954), 52

"The shift in technology caused a shift in farm management as well. Farmers used land formerly devoted to growing feed for horses to plant more wheat and corn. This was not a small shift in production; fully one-sixth of improved acreage on farms had been devoted to growing grain for horses. Direct and indirect demand for these crops had existed, and high market prices had encouraged farmers to grow more during the war. With peace and a rapid return to prewar agricultural consumption levels, the principles of supply and demand dictated poorer cash returns to American food producers. Mortgages and other debts trapped farmers, and the government did not intervene to regulate production by encouraging farmers to take acres out of production. The combination resulted in a decision by a majority of growers to compensate for depressed prices with more output. It would have taken a collective action by a majority of the many millions of producers to reduce supplies enough to have had much positive effect on prices. Foreign-policy decisions favored American industrial interests over those of agriculture. High tariffs hurt farmers, and federal monetary policies discouraged rural investments and loans. Each of these factors either contributed to or deepened the rural depression in the early 1920's."[8]

Small farmers in Indiana had already started down the road to depression in the early1920s. Product was plentiful, prices were low. Indiana and the rest of the nation were years

---

[7] James H. Madison, *Indiana Through Tradition and Change, A History of the Hoosier State and Its People, 1920-1945* Indiana Historical Society , 1982), 164-165

[8] Dennis S. Nordin and Roy V. Scott, *From Prairie Farmer to Entrepreneur, The Transformation of Midwestern Agriculture, (*Indiana University Press 2005), 55

away from any kind of government agricultural subsidies. World War I saw high farm product prices as the government encouraged farmers to over plant and supply the world. The government guaranteed farmers high prices for their crops and their livestock. Farmers cultivated more acres and increased their herds. They borrowed money to buy more land and machinery. Demand for farm land increased and so did its price. By 1919 the Indiana Farm Price Index had doubled the level it was at in 1914.

In 1920 the government ended its guarantees. Farm prices were allowed to drop back naturally. In 1920 as farmers continued to produce more than was needed, the Index fell by half. The Price Index remained low through the 1920s while the cost of goods and services farmers had to buy increased. "Over the course of the twenties, both the net income and the real purchasing power of the farmers declined by 25 percent from the war years and the total value of farm products fell by one half."[9] Those who had borrowed money could not repay their loans. If they sold their farms, they often got less than what was owed. Low prices and high expenses set a depressing tone for farmers.

Small farmers in southern Indiana suffered from more than just economic depression and inability to modernize. Land in the hilly areas of southern Indiana had been overused. Years of planting the same crops in the same fields depleted the soil of needed nitrates. "But in the twenty-three most hilly and unglaciated counties of southern Indiana ... land was converted to pasture, forest, and recreational use (including Brown

---

[9] James H. Madison, *Indiana Through Tradition and Change, A History of the Hoosier State and Its People, 1920-1945* (Indiana Historical Society , 1982), 170

County State Park), but most of it was simply abandoned, as farmers sought employment in towns and cities."[10]

There were other new efficiencies in the 1920's that eluded small farmers and deterred them from profiting from the same improvements their urban neighbors enjoyed. Electricity was bringing people throughout southern Indiana and the Midwest new comforts of living. Census records for 1920 showed that only ten percent of Indiana farms had electric service.

"Stringing power lines to farms was not a priority for Midwest electricity providers. Power companies were reluctant to invest in the lines and transformers that would be capable of bringing electricity to remote customers; in general, they lacked the imagination to envision the tremendous market for electricity that farm businesses represented. They preferred to concentrate on areas with greater population densities or with industrial and commercial consumers. Investor-owned utility companies often required substantial line changes for initial installations to farms and surcharges for connections."[11]

The 1920s presented serious economic difficulties for a lot of farmers including the Langes. "The changes in agriculture that brought prosperity to some forced an end to farming for many others. Most of the productive changes of twentieth-century agriculture were more likely to benefit those with large farms and those whose farms were located on the flat, fertile areas of central and northern Indiana. Small farmers

---

[10] James H. Madison, *Indiana Through Tradition and Change, A History of the Hoosier State and Its People, 1920-1945* (Indiana Historical Society , 1982), 166

[11] Dennis S. Nordin and Roy V. Scott, *From Prairie Farmer to Entrepreneur, The Transformation of Midwestern Agriculture,* (Indiana University Press 2005), 65-66

and those who farmed the hilly, less fertile land of southern Indiana were less able to buy the corn pickers. Indeed, many such farms became marginally profitable at best, kept going only because one or more members of the family had a job off the farm. Many eventually gave up and abandoned the farm for work in town. "[12] The downturn in small farming drove Herman Lange to seek the urban refuge of work. In the city he would find the means to keep his head above water and his family's hold on their farm in Wrights Corner.

Southeastern Indiana farmers watched prices for their products plummet during the agricultural depression. Foreclosure hung like a dark cloud over all farmers. The Lange's found the value of their small farm to be under water. Marc McCutcheon in his book, The *Writer's Guide to Everyday Life From Prohibition Through World War II*, wrote the following. "Many farmers in the Midwest banded together at foreclosure sales by scaring off prospective bidders, buying up all a fellow farmer's valuables for cheap prices, then giving them back to the farmer the next day."[13]

It's not certain if this happened with Herman and Mayme's small farm, but the pages of the Dearborn County Recorder's red bound books show that the farm passed into the name of Judge Charles Lowe in the early 1920's. Herman went to work for the Judge in 1924 quite possibly to enable himself to buy the farm back. The seventy-one acre farm on State Route 48 did again pass into the hands of the Langes on August 30, 1929. The family remained on the farm but did not really

---

[12] James H. Madison, *The Indiana Way, A State History*(Indiana University Press, 1986), 266

[13] Marc McCutheon, *The Writer's Guide to Everyday Life From Prohibition Through World War II,* (Writer's Digest Books, 1995),68

own it through most of the 1920's. Farm Depression weighed them down.

The farmers' inability to modernize and mechanize disturbed Herman and his family. In the early 1920's he began to seek opportunities outside the farm to provide for his family. Being active in the Dearborn County Republican organization aided Herman in his search for a chance to supplement his income and keep the farm going. In 1924 he became riding bailiff for Charles A. Lowe, Judge of the Seventh Judicial Circuit of Dearborn and Ohio Counties.

Lange Farm Deed, August 30, 1929

4

"Rise to Sheriff"

Dad seems happy. He goes to work at the courthouse. He is bailiff for Judge Lowe. Mom says this job will help pay the bills for the farm. She's not happy that he wears a gun to his work.

Stella Mae Lange – *My Journal, 06/12/1924*

Dad going to work in the city feels out of place. I always thought of work as tending to the farm. Up early to feed the horses, feed the cows, milk the cows, feed the chickens, gather eggs, plow the fields, care for the crops, clean the chicken coop, mend the fences all seems like a lot of work to me. I wonder how Dad will go to town and get everything done here at home. Mom now feeds the horses. I feed the chickens and the cows. Mom even teaches me how to milk. I guess that answers my questions. Mom and I will have to pick up some of the slack.

Dad tells me that his new boss, Judge Charles Lowe, runs the proceedings at the courthouse for the Seventh Judicial Circuit of Dearborn and Ohio Counties. That sounds like a real mouthful of nothing. Do they have horses or chickens or cows to attend to at the courthouse? And what does Dad do? Does he have to feed and milk and plow? Dad laughs at my concept of his new work. He can see I really want to know what is so important to take him away so much from me and Mom and our Wrights Corner farm. Dad tells me Judge Lowe is a good man.

~

Judge Lowe was born in Hardentown. He went to Lawrenceburg High School. He attended Depauw University in Greencastle, Indiana, west of Indianapolis. Charles taught in the Guilford Public School for a year after his graduation from college. He found teaching not to his liking, so he enrolled in and completed studies at the Cincinnati YMCA Law School. This school was later to become the Salmon P. Chase School of Law. After graduation Charles took the Ohio Bar Exam. Charles Lowe had the highest grades along with Charles Sawyer of Cincinnati. Lowe's equal in the exam became a storied member of Ohio's legal and political scene.

Sawyer was a member of City Council for Cincinnati from 1912 through 1916. Sawyer was Lieutenant Governor of Ohio from 1933 through 1935, followed by an unsuccessful run for Ohio governor in 1938. He was appointed United States Ambassador to Belgium by Franklin Roosevelt during World War II. He was later United States Secretary of Commerce under Harry Truman From 1948 through 1953. Being equal in the bar exam to Charles Sawyer was pretty impressive company for a small town boy from Hardentown.

Charles Lowe practiced law in Lawrenceburg with Judge Noah Given. It wasn't long until he was appointed to complete the term of deceased Republican Judge of the Seventh Judicial Circuit, Warren Hauck. He won election to a six year term as Circuit Court Judge in 1920.

According to Indiana Law a "judge of the circuit courts in each county having a population of at least thirty-five thousand (35,000) shall appoint a riding bailiff for the Judge's court whose per diem shall be fixed by the court to be paid from the county Treasury." In Indiana a bailiff provides court security. A Circuit Court Judge has a bailiff responsible for calling a jury, seating a jury, as well as attending to a juror's needs. The bailiff is armed and a sworn officer of the court.[14]. In 1924 Judge Lowe taps Herman on the shoulder, "Be my Riding Bailiff."

~

Mom looks at Dad's new job quite differently. Certainly, she thinks Judge Lowe is a fine man and has the reputation as an accomplished judge, but she really questions some of the duties of Dad's new position. However, Mom fears for Dad's safety in executing many of the bailiff's responsibilities. He must chase down and bring to court witnesses and those accused who hesitate to appear before the judge. Mom says there are a lot of bad seeds strewn throughout Dearborn County and Dad will have to travel out to rake them in. He will confiscate property, serve foreclosure notices, collect past due loans, collect unpaid court fines— putting him face to face with down-on-their-luck friends or neighbors. He will encounter a great number of desperate people. Mom doesn't want to lose the farm. More so, she doesn't want to lose Dad. She fears the bailiff to be in potential danger. Mom stiffens her back, but

---

[14] *Indiana Code*, IC 33 - 38 - 2 - 1,
http://codes.lp.findlaw.com/incode/33/38/2/33-38-2-1

understands and complies with the need for Dad to work to save the farm.

As he undertakes his job with Judge Lowe's court, Dad takes a greater interest in politics. Mom and I accompany him to the Republican Party's summer picnics—a good place for me to catch up with all my school chums. I study Dad as he rolls up his sleeves and joins the other men in a game of horseshoes. Dad leans in to their conversations of trouble in the county. He welcomes every opportunity to attend the Republican gatherings in Lawrenceburg. He begins to bring the meetings home to our kitchen table. At night he sits talking to Mom about the happenings throughout Dearborn. I listen with one ear as I try to concentrate on my math homework.

I cherish one of my memories gathered at the Dearborn County Fair. Dad is all business shaking hands and slapping backs. I kinda tag along behind until he makes an abrupt stop at one of the game of chance booths. He urges me to "Watch this," as he takes a mighty toss at a stack of iron milk jugs. The jugs topple. I jump up and down. Dad spies the prizes and picks a special one for me. I now have a special spot on my night stand for a small, gleaming glass elephant. Dad says "It's a Republican." It reminds me every day of good times.

~

Working as bailiff, Herman became increasingly interested in the Republican Party's organization. He was a simple local farmer positioned to impact his county. Change was sadly needed throughout Indiana. There was a general disinterest by the people for the political process of the early 1920's. The roots of this disinterest ran deep.

"World War I left Hoosiers, like other Americans, with an uncertain legacy. Hoosiers seemed as eager as the rest of America to forget the war and to follow President Warren G. Harding's return to "normalcy".[15] The Indiana state populace showed little interest in reform at home. "The postwar decade brought to both major parties a stand-pat perspective."[16]

Another ingredient seasoning the populist's disinterest was political corruption especially at the state level. "The decade's leading politicians, best represented by Senator James E. Watson, seemed little concerned with social and economic problems…, preferring to concentrate on the back-slapping and vote-getting of issueless campaigns and on the backstairs maneuvering of party preferment and organization. "[17] The 1920's saw little positive leadership from either political party. The Ku Klux Klan and Prohibition were two big cesspools of political corruption.

Bankruptcy threatened Warren T. McCray during his term as Indiana governor from 1920 to 1924. He solicited loans via mail to maintain his home and took a questionable loan from the state department of agriculture. The Indiana Attorney General charged McCray with embezzlement. He was tried and sentenced to ten years in federal penitentiary.[18]

Ed Jackson, McCray's successor as governor, was likewise caught in the web of corruption. In 1927 he was

---

[15] James H. Madison, *The Indiana Way, A State History*(Indiana University Press, 1986), 289
[16] James H. Madison, *The Indiana Way, A State History*(Indiana University Press, 1986), 289
[17] James H. Madison, *The Indiana Way, A State History*(Indiana University Press, 1986), 289
[18] James H. Madison, *The Indiana Way, A State History*(Indiana University Press, 1986), 290

investigated and tried on charges of having attempted to bribe the previous governor with money provided him by the Ku Klux Klan. He was not convicted as the statute of limitations had expired. He finished his term in office, but left in disgrace.[19]

Indiana also saw a sharp drop in voter turnout in the 1920's. Corruption and mediocrity may not have been the only cause in the decline of citizen participation, but they were certainly a major cause for this disinterest. The percent of eligible Indiana voters casting ballots in the 1920s was at its lowest ever. The time was right both state wide and in Dearborn County for fresh new faces. Herman Lange was encouraged to bring his bailiff skills to the County Sheriff's Race.

In March of 1924 Herman, encouraged by Judge Lowe, entered the Republican Primary race for sheriff along with J. Chris Lommel of Lawrenceburg. Herman spent a great deal of his free time out in the community putting his name, his face, and his principles before the voters of Dearborn County. On Tuesday, May 6, 1924, the primary elections were held. First time candidate for sheriff, Herman Lange lost by twenty-eight votes, a margin of about one per cent of the total vote. The loss was a bitter pill for Herman to swallow. Would he be persistent and try again, or would this be his last entry into the political arena.

For the next four years Herman digs in and gives the bailiff's job his full attention. He determines he must make twenty-nine new friends in the county to possibly bring a primary win if he returns to the race.

In early 1928, Judge Charles Lowe persuades his bailiff,

---

[19] James H. Madison, *The Indiana Way, A State History*(Indiana University Press, 1986) 290

Herman Lange, to enter the race for Dearborn County Sheriff again. With announcements in both *The Lawrenceburg Press* and *The Lawrenceburg Register*, Herman takes to the campaign trail once again. He is not a lonely candidate. There are three other Republican candidates for Sheriff running in the May primaries. Joe Cunningham, Charles Fauss, and James Hulbert join him on the ballot. Even though there is a light voter turnout for the May 8, 1928 primary, Herman scratches out a victory. He gets 50 percent of the vote and walks away with 100 percent confidence.

~

With the primary win under his belt, Dad races forward dragging me and Mom along. I think I am more willing than she. Starting the eighth grade at Wrights Corner Elementary, I find social studies of particular interest this year as the teacher talks about all the local people on the ballot. I sit up a little straighter in my desk when she talks about the sheriff's race.

Community events and door to door "meet and greets" are the stuff which make a good campaign. Dad takes what time he can from his farm duties and job as bailiff to spread his name around the county. He talks about this being an uphill battle. His Democratic opponent, Frank Winter, is the incumbent sheriff. Although Winter is not an overwhelming favorite in the race, he has certainly not done anything to bring question to his ability to perform the job of sheriff.

Mom, with clear eyes, pushes Dad to go after women's votes. It has not been that many years since the 19th Amendment gave women the right to vote. Leave it to Mom to overturn every stone. She votes each year and advocates for her friends and neighbors to do the same. She uses her fiery spirit to drive Dad to talk with the women as well as the men after Sunday services. Mom even arranges for Dad to speak to her Daughters of America group. It's strange to see Mom fight so hard to help Dad win a job that she fears so much.

On October 4, 1928, I run out to the mail box looking for the latest *Lawrenceburg Press.* Dad told me this was coming, but I am still excited about an endorsement appearing in the "Who's Who in Dearborn County" section of the paper. Written by Robert Reed, the article paints a glowing portrait of Dad. I clip the piece and save it inside my scrapbook.

~

"This particular sketch may take on the appearance of being a political story, but, as a matter of fact, it is not. It happens, because of the arrangement of selecting persons for this department that Herman Lange, who lives in Manchester Township, is a candidate for sheriff of Dearborn County.

The Herman Lange of this sketch was born in York Township, September 3, 1889, the son of William and Louise (Lampe) Lange. He started to school at Wrights Corner, moving with his parents for a while to Elizabethtown, returning to Manchester Township after a period of two years, where he has resided since that time.

After his early school days, he worked on his parents' farm, as so many native born Dearborn County boys have done, mixing in the social life of their communities to such an extent that they feel that there is no place better than Dearborn County, (and the writer agrees with them) and on November 29, 1911 he was married to Mayme Gesell, daughter of John and Anna Mary (Franzman) Gesell. A daughter (Stella), aged 14, a pupil in the Aurora High School is the result of this union.

Four years ago, Mr. Lange was riding bailiff under Judge Lowe, Lawrenceburg. He is now, and has always operated a farm in Manchester Township, considerable fruit being products of his farm.

He is next to the eldest of a family of seven. Will, the eldest, lives at Hartford City; Tillie, a sister, is the wife of Roy Bennett, Muncie; Alpha, living at Greendale; Dora, the wife of Elmer Smith, Aurora; Mary, wife of George W. McDowell, Big Four passenger agent at Lawrenceburg and Manchester Township.

Since Mr. Lange is the Republican nominee for sheriff, a story of one of his acts recently in which he brought two automobile thieves to justice, would not be out of place. Mr. Lange single-handed caught two culprits at Manchester and brought them to the County seat where they were turned over to the officers. The Press and other newspapers of Dearborn County at the time commended the young man for his valor because of the capture.

The name of Lange is a well-known one in the history of Indiana. It goes without saying that he would make a good, clean, conscientious public official and would unquestionably serve all the people, in the event he was elected, to the best of his ability.

Mr. Lange is a church member, a total abstainer, and thoroughly in accord with the Indiana and National prohibition laws, and h quiet, peaceful life gives proof to all his friends and others who are interested that there is naught but good could come from his official acts if ac corded a place of official honor by the voters of Dearborn County."[20]

Herman Lange Sheriff of Dearborn County, Indiana
Herman's Republican affiliation helps his battle for votes. The party's message resonates with the people of the county. Herbert Hoover, Republican candidate for President, is a popular choice over Democratic, anti-Prohibition, Catholic

[20] Robert Reed, "Who's Who," *The Lawrenceburg Press*, 04 October 1928

Alfred Smith. Mayme assures Herman that he will be a part of the Republican remedy in fall elections. He appeals strongly to his constituents, vowing to fight against the evils of prohibition that rain down upon Dearborn County

In the November 1928 election Hoover wins in a landslide. In Dearborn County seventy per cent of the vote goes to Hoover. Herman has a margin of 629 votes over Democratic incumbent Frank Winter.

~

 I pose a collection of miniature glass elephants prominently atop my dresser. I add to the menagerie honoring Republicans every chance I get.

Mom and I enjoy Dad's win. With his promise to serve the people of the county, Dad will take on the myriad duties of an Indiana County Sheriff. Mom says his time as Bailiff in the county's circuit court prepared him well for the job he will soon undertake.

We are ill prepared for the move. I guess I never expected Dad to win. I knew if he won we would have to move from the farm to the jail house. The realization of moving is a shock. I love the farm. My feet root firmly in the rich red mud.

Mom won't let me fret. She says, "Get up and get over it. Move on!" These are hard words for fourteen-year-old me to accept, but Mom leaves no choice. Judge Lowe begins searching for a renter to care for the farm while Dad holds his office. They find a renter and we prepare for the move.

5

"Prohibition"

I don't understand all the fuss about Prohibition. The pastor on Sunday says alcohol is bad for us. Mom and Dad don't drink. If drinking is such a poor choice why do so many people do it?
Stella Mae Lange – *My Journal, 01/17/1928*

I learn about Prohibition in Freshman Civics class at Aurora High School. Mom frets that the criminal push to side-step Prohibition poses a big problem for Dad if he becomes sheriff. All of us know about the riff-raff in West Harrison along the Whitewater River camps. We pass the area on trips to see Mom's Gesell relatives in Brookville. Dad turns home before the sun goes down, because a lot of bad people doing a lot of bad things infest the area along that river. So, my ears perk up and I pay attention to the Civics lessons. I want to know what is happening and what Dad will face.

I come home from school and sit down with Mom to tell her what I am learning in Civics class. She listens attentively though she probably already knows everything about Prohibition. Mom is pretty smart that way.

~

On January 16, 1919, the 36th state ratified the 18th amendment to the Constitution of the United States. After years of rallies, protests, political action this grand experiment became the law of the land. Activists sold it to the public as a means to reduce crime and corruption, solve social problems, reduce taxes needed for police and prisons, and improve public health. The Volstead act made enforcement of prohibition effective on January 16, 1920. Across the United States 177,000 saloons, 1900 breweries, and 236 distilleries were closed. The country went dry. The nightmare of enforcement of prohibition disturbed every sheriff's sleep.

Prohibition created more problems than it solved. Strict policing of Prohibition failed to keep people from bypassing the law. Consumption of alcohol fell in the beginning of the Volstead act's enforcement. Alcohol consumption increased 500 percent since 1921. Normal citizens seeking alcohol helped foster a new criminal element. Prohibition's desired goal to reduce criminal activity was drowned under a sea of illegal liquor. Jails were packed and courts clogged with Prohibition violators.

Prohibition had a negative effect on the death rate. Not only was bootlegging illegal, it was dangerous. On New Year's Day, 1927, scores of people were admitted to New York's Bellevue Hospital. Forty-one of those people died, all from poisonous liquor. In 1926 in New York City there were 750 such deaths. Although there are no statistics to support it, by 1927 there were probably over 50,000 deaths related to poisonous liquor in the United States. Nonfatal cases resulting in paralysis, blindness, kidney failure, and other diseases likely numbered in the hundreds of thousands.

~

A lot of kids doze off with all these statistics, but my ears perk up. I want to know what ills Dad will battle. Some of the Lawrenceburg papers are references that our teacher uses in class. He tells us that the local papers are filled with stories of moonshining, bootlegging, and hijacking of both legal and illegal liquor throughout the 1920's.

~

The Sheriff raided a farm finding 100 bottles of moonshine on Guilford Road near Homestead. In another instance, police investigating a shooting found a supply of corn mash and a still.

    The Rossville Distilling Company had a truck hijacked in June, 1921. The truck with Melvin Walker of Aurora driving was held up at the Anderson Ferry as it neared Cincinnati. Walker was tied up by 6 men and thrown in the back of the truck. Rossville enlisted Ora Slater, a Lawrenceburg native and Cincinnati detectives to recover the stolen alcohol. Herman had invited Mr. Slater, previously Dearborn County Sheriff, to solicit help in the sheriff's campaign.

    Numerous accounts in *The Lawrenceburg Press* told of unlawful stills, illegal sales of intoxicating liquor. June, 1923, Sheriff Winters discovered a still near Homestead by Tanners Creek. He found the still when investigating shots fired at a group of men fishing in the creek. Apparently the men were too close to the still. This was one of the largest unlawful stills in the county. It was dismantled and taken to the jail

~

This was another story of interest to me. If elected, Dad will replace Sheriff Winters. Dad will be investigating a still somewhere in the county. This lands too close to hom. Mom doesn't like this story much either.

Another lesson in civics concerning Prohibition rings a very familiar bell. Dad became bailiff and then would run for sheriff because the farm could not support our family. I sit up straight and take notes when the teacher talks about Prohibition's effect on farmers.

~

With agriculture being a big part of Indiana's economy, the state's farmers produced a lot of grain. Overproduction of grain in the 1920's contributed heavily to farm depression. The Volstead Act "dried up a major market for hops, barley, corn, rye, and other crops used in brewing beer and distilling alcoholic spirits. Farmers resorted to growing more acres of oversupplied field crops, thus glutting even more what had already become a saturated supply of certain foodstuffs."[21]

Corn plays a major role in Indiana agriculture. In 1910 census records Indiana produced 195,496,433 bushels of corn ranking third in the United States. In 1925, the height of Prohibition, corn production fell almost fifty per cent to 99,853,733 bushels ranking sixth across the land. Even the

[21] Dennis S. Nordin and Roy V. Scott, *From Prairie Farmer to Entrepreneur, The Transformation of Midwestern Agriculture,* (Indiana University Press 2005), 55

"dry" state, Indiana, was a key player in liquor production.

~

Mom listens quietly to my retelling of Civics class lessons. Finally, she says, "Stella, these are all reasons your Father should not become sheriff. Problems of Prohibition will make his job difficult. It will make his job very dangerous. I don't want him to do this, but I will not stand in his way. He has taken good care of you and me. He feels that the sheriff's job presents a means for him to continue to take care of us. I only pray that he will take good care of himself as well."

Mom goes to her bedroom and brings out an old newspaper to show to me. "I keep this in the bottom of my drawer" she says. "I save it because I know the man in the story. He grew up in my hometown of Brookville. He and his wife knew the Gesells very well. I bring the paper out whenever my mind becomes dulled to the dangers of a sheriff's job. It shakes me back to reality. I don't belabor your Father with the article and I don't expect you to bother him with it either. I do want you to know, however, why the sheriff's duty scares me." With that she showed me a tattered front page from *The Brookville Democrat* dated August 23, 1923, and told me this story

~

There was one area of Dearborn County and nearby Franklin County that was particularly infested with the ills of Prohibition. Along the Whitewater River in the southwestern part of the counties were criminal nests infected with the illegal liquor, gambling, and questionable women. Old run down cabins and resort homes that were once peaceful summer retreats along the meandering flow of the Whitewater River offered out of the way speakeasies tucked astride a gravel and mud path. These "camps" tore at the fabric of a community devoted to the good of Prohibition. They were a law enforcement nightmare.

One southeastern Indiana law enforcement death in 1923 was tied to the evils of bootlegging. Sheriff William Van Camp of Franklin County, Indiana, was shot and killed in the line of duty on August 20, 1923. The sheriff was shot while investigating a pair of suspicious characters sitting on the running board of their car in a field near Brookville, Indiana. *The Brookville Democrat* recounted the story of Sheriff Van Camp's murder. While running Jack Daniel's whiskey from St. Louis to Cincinnati, George Remus was purported to have killed Sheriff William Van Camp near Brookville, Indiana. Though George Remus was implicated in the murder, no one was ever brought to trial for the deed. These were dangerous and frightening times for any law enforcement officer even in the small rural communities of southeastern Indiana.

~

"Your Father will be in danger as sheriff. The newspaper reminds me of that always."

6

"Herman Term as Sheriff Dearborn County"
No one asked me if I wanted to move to Lawrenceburg. We traded a nice big farm for a small white house…a jailhouse. Maybe the kids at Aurora High School won't realize I live in jail.

Stella Mae Lange – *My Journal, 12/30/1928*

On January 1, 1929, a small ceremony in Judge Charles Lowe's chambers begins Dad's term as Sheriff of Dearborn County. The judge, Dad, Mom, and I are the only people present. No fanfare, no drum rolls, no flowery speeches greet us. Dad puts on his badge. Our lives change.

Herman Lange's Sheriff Badge

~

The following note of thanks and declaration of dedication to duty from Herman Lange appeared in the Lawrenceburg Press following his election. "I desire to express my deep appreciation to the voters of Dearborn County who chose me to be their sheriff. I promise equal justice to all in the administration of this office, and that I will, to the utmost of my ability preserve law and order during my tenure of service."

With his promise to serve the people of the county, Herman took on the myriad duties of an Indiana County Sheriff. His time as Bailiff in the county's circuit court prepared him well for the job he was about to undertake. He was empowered to arrest persons committing an offense, take them before the court of the county, and detain them until an investigation of an arrest had been made. Keeping the peace, pursuing and jailing felons, executing judicial process, preserving order in all courts of the county, caring for the jailed prisoners all fell under the umbrella of a county sheriff's duties.[22]

Mayme would be called upon to share in the sheriff's work with her keen record keeping skills honed through years of managing the finances on their small farm. She helped Herman provide an accounting to the state corrections department for the costs of housing prisoners in the county.[23]

As Sheriff he was to provide his own badge, his own gun, his own ammunition, his own transportation. The reward in the job of sheriff would be that of a job well done, and not

---

[22] http://en.wikipedia.org/wiki/County_sheriff
[23] Ind. Code 36-2-13-16.3

monetary compensation as the salary was only $183.33 per month.

The following "Lawrenceburg Press" article introducing Herman's term as Sheriff is more than a little prophetic of what might come.

"Then there comes the County Sheriff, Mr. Frank Winters, a very agreeable citizen. But it seems the voters were not in accord for a third termer and as he had already served two terms, he was defeated by his old opponent, Herman Lange.

Mr. Lange is another farmer, his life having been spent in a farm near the Bellair Church. There he worked and toiled from the years of his boyhood days until one day as he was plowing in the field he was stung by the office seeking bug, and he never more could be contented until he announced himself as a candidate for County Sheriff.

Defeat had no sorrows for him, for no sooner defeated than he was up and going again and the last time he made the race in earnest so that he went over with a big majority

Mr. Lange, sheriff of Dearborn County, took his office New Year's Day. From the general makeup of Mr. Lange we judge that he will serve with honor for the next two years having only one thing in mind, that is that he has been elected sheriff of Dearborn County and will make the supreme effort of his life to grace the office with honor, with naught but equal and exact justice for all. [24]

~

The call to duty this swearing in represents does not affect Dad

---

[24] *The Lawrenceburg Press*, 02 January 1929, 1

alone. He is the elected sheriff. He will serve the people of Dearborn County. Mom and I are carried along, not elected but affected just the same. We are uprooted. We are moved from our comfortable farm in Wrights Corner to the house and jail on High Street in the city of Lawrenceburg. Our new home rests at on 310 West High Street in downtown Lawrenceburg.

Dearborn County Jailhouse

The big square white frame and stucco house sits just southwest of the courthouse. It has two bedrooms upstairs. My bedroom has a big window giving me a birds-eye view of High Street. The living room and dining room are on the first floor. The kitchen lies toward the back of the same floor with a thick padlocked door adjoining the jail. The padlock doesn't dissuade my fears of escaping prisoners.

Dad's sheriff's office sits in the front of the building. Four small cells for prisoners occupy the area behind the office. In the cells, dusty old wood-slatted bunk beds hang by chain from the block walls. Each room offers a small, enamel wash basin.

There are two big wood-burning stoves, one in the home, one in the jail. January attacks us already and these stoves' fires are lit in rooms that inhale winter through wheezing walls and windows. Indoor plumbing in the sheriff's office and in the house proffers a welcome novelty for us. No such convenience availed itself to us at the farm. No more cold winter morning walks.

Strange sounds attack my ears the very first night in my jailhouse bed. I can't make out the origin of the unfamiliar noises, or even know what they purport. Scratches like metal on brick. Rasps like a dog gnawing a bone. Wheezes like a horse grasping for breath. Moans like a cry from the dead. I sit up in bed, wide-eyed, teeth grinding, feet and hands cold as a sick calf. I call to Mom. She begs me to ignore and sleep. I shake the sounds out of myself like a wet dog. Dad's term is for two years. Will I make it?

By light of day, Mom seizes the job of jail's Matron, a Dearborn County tradition for a Sheriff's wife. She will keep all the sheriff's books. She will cook and feed all prisoners. She will keep records for reimbursement of expenses for meals and department transportation. She will tend to cleaning and maintenance of the jail. Mom cooks for the prisoners. She assures all the sheriff's county records to be accurate. I always knew Mom was good at everything she did.

I dig my heels in and protest, but I am still responsible at times to help feed those prisoners. I began my freshman year in high school in 1928 at Aurora High School. I really enjoyed school there. A lot of my friends from up on the horn attended school there also. Even with the move to Lawrenceburg Jail mid school year, Mom says I can stay in school at Aurora to finish the year. I'll ride a street car from Lawrenceburg each day. I enjoy that trip. Maybe I'll join choir.

I am okay with Dad's new job, not thrilled but just okay. Mom is not at all happy. I see her as pleasant and positive around Dad, but not so with me. As I get older, Mom talks to me more. She tells me her concerns. She says Prohibition's demand for bootleg liquor has increased disrespect for the law. The Farm Depression proves to be an incentive for increased criminal activities across the state. Press, radio and movies sensationalize crime and encourage its growth.

Mom grumbles, "Just look at the movies at the Walnut Theatre in Lawrenceburg." She shares what she hears from ladies after church services saying, "Lon Chaney in *The Big City* has guns, robberies, murders throughout the film. Crime is glamorized. I don't understand it."

Mom talks about the problems automobiles pose. She growls, "The growing popularity of affordable automobiles flaunts a nightmare of problems before local lawmen. Stolen cars, speeding, robbery getaways, fender-benders pepper front pages of local newspapers. Henry Ford made the automobile affordable for everyone. Cars speeding recklessly over the unregulated highways are steel death traps. A sheriff using his own automobile fights a losing battle containing the problems the automobile drives at him." Blunt-faced Mom observes, "These times facing any sheriff, inexperienced, poorly equipped, lack of law enforcement savvy, write a recipe for disaster. Dad is in for trouble."

Mom goes about her business as matron like everything she does—detailed, thorough, and dedicated. She studies every entry made in the county sheriff's arrest log. She even saves a few more newspaper clippings to track Dad's activities. The first couple of months of Dad's term are rather uneventful. The calm breaks beginning in March. Mom clips a newspaper article from *The Lawrenceburg Register* of March 28, 1929 detailing a story of thieves making a big haul.

~

Thieves entered the residence of Mr. and Mrs. Elmer Oelker on Ludlow Hill during their absence Sunday evening and stole goods to the value of about $275.

Entrance was gained through a side window, which was unlocked. Articles taken included men's wearing apparel, dresser sets, pearl necklace, radio and batteries, forty chickens, two clocks and a number of other articles.

When Mr. and Mrs. Oelker returned home about nine o'clock they noticed two handkerchiefs lying on the front porch, which the thieves had dropped. This made them suspicious and when they entered their home and took a survey of things were soon aware of what had happened.

Neighbors saw the light from a machine in the yard early in the evening but thinking Mr. and Mrs. Oelker had returned home, paid no attention to it. Tracks near the house showed that the culprits had carried the goods some distance from the house and loaded it into a car.

The same evening thieves entered the home of Carl Ligget between Lawrenceburg Junction and the State Line and stole some wearing apparel. In leaving the Ligget home some of the apparel was also dropped in the yard. It is thought that the same thieves robbed the two homes.[25]

~

---

[25] *The Lawrenceburg Register,* 28 March 1929, 1

There is more activity as Dad's year in office continues. Mom clips another article from *The Lawrenceburg Press* of June 20, 1929 relating another crime. Her scrapbook must be getting full. She saves everything written about Dad.

~

The Whippet sedan of Chas. Zimmer of Kelso was stolen from Walnut Street of this city on Sunday night. The same evening the license plates were stolen from the car of David Criswe

    On Monday morning Mr. Zimmer reported the theft to Sheriff Lange. Shortly after this the sheriff received word from Fred Schwing, at Harrison, that deputy sheriffs had found a machine, when making their rounds at a gravel pit on the Campbell Road southeast of Harrison. As the car bore an Indiana license it was towed to the Schwing barbecue near the Harrison Bridge. Sheriff Lange went to Harrison and found that it was the one stolen here Sunday night. The license plates stolen from Criswell's car were on the Zimmer machine, from which the thieves had removed the front tires and rims. Other removable parts of the car were not taken.[26]

~

Despite Mom's fear for Dad's well-being, he always cajoles her to believe he is safe. Dad often notes that he is mired in the swamp formed of the ills of the new and easy ownership of the automobile. His old farm truck, a 1917 ½ ton Ford Model T Road Truck with its 22.5 horsepower, is no match for the many

---

[26] *The Lawrenceburg Press,* 20 June, 1929

new vehicles zooming around the roads of Dearborn County. Though he can ill afford the purchase, Dad decides to catch up to the auto-linked offenders. His safety depends upon keeping up with the bad guys. He convinces Mom of the need. He buys a new 1929 Hupmobile S model sedan in October. I like it better than the truck. I would still prefer to have Blackie on the farm.

Dad does not spend all his time chasing speeders and tracking stolen merchandise. A big event coming in October, 1929 will certainly tax Dad's sheriff ability. President Herbert Hoover plans a whistle stop through Lawrenceburg. Mom and I both know that security for such an important public figure must present big headaches. Protecting the people of Dearborn County is a massive task in itself. Protecting the President of the United States is an overwhelming task.

~

The Lawrenceburg Register account of Herbert Hoover's visit on October 29, 1929, shows good luck shining on Herman in his task of protecting the President. The trees are draped in October gray. The wind pulses wintry along the river. Rain spits down in flurries Bad weather keeps the President's steam ship on the river heading for a stop only in Cincinnati.

Tuesday was one of the most disagreeable days that we have had in many months. Several thousand people were in Lawrenceburg to welcome President Hoover...on his voyage down the Ohio....Hundreds stood on the river bank in a cold drizzling rain ...awaiting ...a glimpse of the boat bearing the Chief Executive as it rounded the bend in the river near Columbia power plant...The assembled crowd was enthusiastic in its greeting and with their cheers, blowing of whistles, the firing of the President's salute and the band playing, the people soon forgot the weather and all eyes were strained to catch a glimpse of President Hoover.[27]

~

Mom says, "Prohibition, the Depression, and the Automobile have dropped numerous and novel problems into Dad's lap. No light illuminates the end of the tunnel for the remainder of his term.

---

[27] *The Lawrenceburg Register, 29 October 1929, 1*

7

"Trouble at the Bootleg Camps"

I will never be able to accept being awakened in the middle of the night. There can be no good news coming with the shrill ring of the phone at two a.m. Where is Dad?
Stella Mae Lange – *My Journal, 12/30/1929*

December 29, we drive from the jail house to attend Sunday services at the Manchester Lutheran Church. I love church services at St. Stephen. The small white church, its steeple rising above the front door, warms and welcomes all. I don't know if it's the fresh stoked fire in the big, black pot-belly stove near the front of the church or the sight of so many familiar faces in the pews that warms me more. Today Christmas vacation excites me. I haven't seen many of my Aurora friends in over a week.

After the final 'Amen,' Dad stands on the church steps, arms folded across his chest talking to James Hulbert and some other men I don't know. I overhear their conversation about the young boy from Rhode Island who stole a Sanitary Cleaning Company truck and in his escape drove into the bridge in Newton. Dad caught the lad and brought him to the jail before taking him to Judge Ricketts. I thought he was cute, not like so many of the hooligans who pass through the jail. Cute or not, the boy went before the judge and got to spend time at the reformatory at Pendleton. Dad spent most of Wednesday delivering him.

Mom's on the other side of the church steps gabbing with her Daughters of America friends. They discuss a little politics, but I turn a deaf ear to most of their conversations. I hear them approve of President Hoover's immigration plans. I don't understand and I allow it to fall out of my head.

I seek out Ginny and Maggie. I want to hear what they've been doing during Christmas break. I know there have been some good movies at the Walnut, but Dad was gone a couple of evenings and Mom made me stay home. Aurora plays Lawrenceburg in basketball next week. We girls plan to attend. I know we will sit on Aurora's side.

Church services over, we head back down the hill for a restful Sunday lingering over the remaining joys of the Christmas Holiday. Mom takes advantage of the near empty jail house to cook us a fine chicken dinner. Mom and Dad retire to the living room to listen to the radio. I am lucky enough to talk my friends into seeing a movie. This is a wonderful ending to a too quick vacation.

At two a.m. Monday morning, the clanging ring of the phone shakes us from our sleep. Fred Schwing, who lives near the Harrison Bridge, calls Dad telling him that a man has been shot. I wake just enough to take in this much. My senses soon dull over and I fall asleep again. From this point the early morning is all a fog-like dream to me.

~

The shooting took place at a bootleg camp on the Whitewater River, a no man's land on the Ohio and Indiana border from which law enforcement of either state or county is far removed. The Barn Camp is run by a man named "Spike". The shooting victim is Ben Shaw, 68, of Connersville, Indiana.

Following Fred Schwing's early morning phone call, Herman and his deputy, Lafe Perpington, drive to the scene of the disturbance. It is a hard twenty minute drive along dark and winding State Line Road that leads to a desolate area of West Harrison. The camps along the Whitewater River are dens of sin and corruption. Prohibition has laid this area wide open to the evils of liquor, gambling, and sex tempting the citizens of Dearborn and other nearby counties.

Arriving at "Spike's" camp, Herman and Lafe find the shooting victim, Ben Shaw, has already been treated by Dr. Schoenling of Harrison and transported to Cincinnati's Good Samaritan Hospital. The sheriff and his deputy briefly investigate the events and question the suspects, Gus Seiter and Roscoe Bradburn.

The pair of lawmen cuff Seiter and Bradburn and load them in Herman's Hupmobile. They hurry back to the jail. The sheriff wants to get back on the road to search for the fleeing gunman.

~

I rub the sleep from my eyes catching a glimpse of Dad and Lafe bringing two men into the jail. Mom's eyes flare like a struck match. I hear Dad tell her that Lafe will hold the men in jail so he can get back on the road to unravel the crime. Mom and I, having already been awakened by the two a. m. phone call of trouble, are now sure to have a sleepless night. Dad, in a rush to capture the shooter from the camp, asks Mom to record his prisoners in the Sheriff's Log Book. She agrees but asks first that he allow her to fix the button on his worn wool coat. He says no. I reach out to hug him as he leaves, but instead I catch and tear the loose button. It falls to the floor. Dad hesitates for a second but rushes out to find the fleeing gunman. I want to wait and watch for his return, but my heavy eyes urge me back to bed.

~

Herman, weary and alone, is out into the early morning mist. The sheriff heads along the Harrison/Brookville Road in search of James Anderson, the drunken, angry shooter from the camp. He stops briefly in Brookville to share a cup of coffee and information with Franklin County Sheriff Personett. With miles to search for the fleeing suspect, Herman heads south along the dark road. There are no street lights. The moon hides behind dark clouds obscuring the hunter's vision. Both sides of the two lane blacktop road are fenced by corn fields covered with winter's decay. The Hupmobile's windows are down— Herman's eyes, stung by the cold, December, night air search the side of the road for the fugitive. Few houses dot the road and pop up only every few miles.

The cool, damp winds bite at Herman's uncovered skin. The rain's mist brushes across the cold waters of the Whitewater River, stirring up a heavy, chilly, fog that blankets the fields and crawls up and over the railroad tracks spilling across the highway. Herman struggles to see the road. He drives further and further down the road, finding no one along the fog covered path.

A cold, misty, starless night, riding along a deserted country road, is the stuff of which "film noir" is made. But this is no movie. Knowing that a scared, fleeing gunman is waiting somewhere along the road, makes Herman's heart race. How easy would it be to turn that Hupmobile around and return to seek help capturing the fugitive? Daylight, deputies, friends, a posse are all reasons to turn around. Mayme and Stella waiting at the jail house are reason enough to turn around. Herman does not turn around. He continues down the road. What drives him on? Upon taking office he made a vow to Dearborn County citizens in the November 15, 1928 edition of *The Lawrenceburg Press* promising, "I promise equal justice in the administration of this office. I will, to the utmost of my ability, preserve law and order during my tenure of service."[28]

Longenecker Station
It is almost five a.m. on the still, dark, damp road.

---

[28] *The Lawrenceburg Press,* 15 November 1928

Herman spots the shooter not far from the scene of the crime near Braysville and the Longenecker rail station. He stops his car to question the man on the embankment. The sheriff's buttonless coat blows open revealing his gold badge to the stranger. The man is James Anderson, the young shooter at "Spike's" bootleg camp. He is an arm's length from Herman. Fearful, the stranger draws his gun and fires two shots at Herman. One bullet strikes the sheriff's hand, the second passes through his stomach, penetrating his intestines. As he falls wounded, the sheriff empties six desperate shots from his weapon, one striking the stranger's shoulder. Herman lay bleeding on the road.

The sheriff watches Anderson flee across the road. The gunman scurries across rain slicked railroad tracks, tumbles down a dirt and gravel embankment, and disappears into the nearby corn field. The scared shooter follows this path of river, railroad, corn field and highway all the way to Brookville and then Connersville in a frantic search for friend or family to aid him.

Herman rolls off the highway onto the wet graveled grass of the embankment. The warmth of blood flowing from his wounds is soon chased by the chill of fear and shock. His heart tells him he needs to reach Mayme and Stella. His mind tells him he has a duty to follow the running suspect. Herman's body tells him death is imminent if he fails to find aid now. He fights mightily with the pain, fear, and loneliness draining his body and soul.

Herman struggles to get up, his serious wounds leadening his feet. He drags himself to a nearby farm house. He calls for help but no one answers. Just a few hours earlier there had been a flurry of activity in the area. Partiers fled the speakeasy, the wounded patron was taken to a Cincinnati hospital, the shooter's accompli were jailed in Lawrenceburg, and the gunman fled through the fields. The sheriff is the lone player left on the stage of this tragedy. He is bleeding badly as his blood stains the seat of his car and drenches his coat.

After a time that seems like forever to the wounded sheriff, a light flickers in the house shining on a man in the doorway. The farmer does not recognize the sheriff and hesitates to help him, thinking Herman has wandered to his door from the nearby camps. Blood stained and groggy, Herman pleads his case convincing the puzzled farmer that he is Sheriff of Dearborn County.

The farmer, Thomas Maines, helps Herman into the house. In the yellow light of the hallway bulb, the man sees that Herman's wounds are serious. He calls for Doctor Sheets who quickly assesses that the sheriff's condition is grave. Herman lays suffering on the farmhouse sofa. The ambulance of the Jackman and Penny Funeral Home of Harrison returns, after a time that seems to be forever, to transport the sheriff to Cincinnati's Bethesda Hospital. There doctors work feverishly, hopeful for Herman's recovery. The hopes are short-lived.

What a difference time makes. A few seconds spent differently by either Herman or James Anderson on this fateful morning would dramatically change what happened to each of these men. Even the smallest of change in what each man did or didn't do, consciously or unconsciously, that dreary December morning could have altered how each would spend the rest of his life. If Herman had allowed Mayme the time to repair his loose coat button, would he have avoided the fugitive? If Herman had one more cup of coffee with Sheriff Personett as he stopped at Brookville, would he not encounter the shooter on the road? The window of fate for the men crossing paths was only open a crack. Choices were made and the two collided. The window was thrown wide open. Sheriff Herman Lange lay dying at a remote farm in Dearborn County.

~

It's six a.m. I think I'm awake. I can see Mom's pale, drawn, bloodless face as she listens to some stranger talking to her about Dad. I strain to hear what he is saying. My mind is still in a foggy sleep as I grasp at the words "sheriff", "shot", "escaped", "hospital". Mom quickly urges me to prepare for school. She directs me to dress and catch the street car at the corner by seven a.m. With those hurried instructions, Mom is off with James Hulbert to a hospital in Cincinnati.

I leave for school. I get little explanation of what is happening. My desk may as well be empty; my mind is not in school.

I return from school in the afternoon. Mom is still not back. One of Dad's sisters, Dora Smith, comes to stay with me. I am a teenager. I don't need someone to look after me. I need someone to tell me what is going on. Perhaps, the newspaper might offer the information I seek.

~

The Lawrenceburg Press January 2, 1930, edition recounts the story of the shooting at the bootleg camp. *James Anderson, 20, Gus Seiter, 30, and Roscoe Bradburn, 30, all of Brookville, who were at the reputed homebrew place, became boisterous and unruly, and were ordered from the place, when it is alleged Anderson pulled his gun and threatened to shoot anyone who molested him. A few minutes later the three men left the place and just before driving away in their car, five or six bullets were fired into the building. One of the balls which passed through the door struck Shaw in the thigh, inflicting a serious wound.*[29]

The January 2, 1930, edition of *The Lawrenceburg Register* details more of the morning's activities. *The three young men who precipitated the trouble came down from Franklin County Sunday night and went to a camp known as "The Barn". Here they tried to start trouble, but were unsuccessful. Leaving here they proceeded a short distance down the road to the camp operated by a man known as "Spike". Here they also tried to start a fight and the proprietor of the place seeing the gun on one of the men, quietly took it away from him. When the men started to leave the place the gun was returned to Anderson who seemed the most peaceable of the trio. Just as soon as they were on the outside, Anderson fired the gun, the bullet passing through the door and through the upper part of the leg of Benjamin Shaw, 68, Connersville, who was just closing the door when struck. After the shooting Anderson disappeared but his two companions remained near the scene of the shooting.*[30]

Still another account of the evenings events on the Whitewater River come from the January 2, 1930 *The Aurora Press. One version of the trouble which started the fatal shooting is that the three young men who precipitated the trouble came down from Franklin County to a place known as "The Barn". They were unsuccessful in starting trouble there*

[29] *The Lawrenceburg Press,* 02 January 1930, 1
[30] *The Lawrenceburg Register,* 02 January 1930, 1

and proceeded to the point known as "Spike's camp." Here they again started trouble and the proprietor, seeing that one of the men carried a gun, quietly took it away from him. Before the trio left, the gun was returned to Anderson, and as they left the camp, a shot was fired through the door, supposedly by Anderson. Benjamin Shaw, 68, Connersville, Indiana, was closing the camp door when the bullet struck him in the leg. He was rushed to the Good Samaritan Hospital (Cincinnati, Ohio), where he is recovering from the wound. Anderson disappeared from the scene of the shooting and when the officers arrived only the two companions were found. The section where the shooting occurred has long been known to county authorities in both Indiana and Ohio as a rendezvous for liquor runners. Raids have occurred frequently there, while not at the camp where Monday's trouble commenced, but at other places nearby, but no fights have been recorded by the sheriffs or their deputies.[31]

The Brookville Democrat unfolds this tale of the night's events. *James Anderson, employed on a farm near Brookville, in company with Gus Seiter and Roscoe Bradburn, of this city visited an alleged beer camp on the Whitewater River, near Harrison, Sunday night. The three quarreled after drinking liquor at the camp, it is charged, and during the argument Anderson was said to have fired four shots through the door, one shot wounding Benjamin Shaw, 62, of Connersville, a bystander.*

Sheriff Lange was summoned and he and a deputy arrived at the camp. Anderson had disappeared when the sheriff arrived, Seiter and Bradburn were taken to the Lawrenceburg jail.

---

[31] *The Aurora Press*, 02 January 1930,

Lange continued to hunt for Anderson, coming to Brookville, and on his return toward Lawrenceburg, he met Anderson who it is said drew a gun and fired without warning, two shots striking the sheriff in the abdomen. Lange is said to have retaliated with six shots.

It is reported Anderson had been seen at a residence in this city (Brookville) Wednesday night and a posse was quickly formed hunting for the man, but no trace of the slayer could be found.

Mr. Lange was well known in this county (Franklin), having a number of relatives in the Klemme's Corner neighborhood.[32]

~

I am frightened. My eyes can barely steady on the black print. Newspapers don't tell me what is happening. Aunt Dora can't tell me. I must see Mom. I must see Dad.

---

[32] *The Brookville Democrat,* 02 January 1930, 1

8

"End of Watch"

Dad's in the hospital. Aunt Dora has been staying with me. Mom is gone most of the time. I want to see Dad.

Stella Mae Lange – *My Journal, 12/30/1929*

School is a waste today. My mind is anywhere but math class. I am glad when school is out and I can get home for news of Dad. Mom has not returned from the hospital in Cincinnati yet. Aunt Dora is still here with me. Deputy Lafe Perpington's wife has come also to help at the jail. Two of the people who had been at the Whitewater camp with the man who shot Dad are now in the jail. Someone needs to tend to them. I will not. As far as I'm concerned, the jail could blow up and I wouldn't care. All I want is to have Dad back safe.

Mom returns home. She gives me what news she has. Doctor E. B. Shewman performed emergency surgery on Dad. Doctors are hopeful as Dad continues to cling to life. She says he was quiet after the surgery but still did not look good.

Mom talks to Lafe and Hulbert as a crowd gathers outside our house on the courthouse lawn. There is a large posse of men gathered to search for Dad's attacker.

~

Hulbert has some concerns as some faces in the crowd shout for justice and grumble and mumble about Seiter and Bradburn, friends of the shooter, sitting nearby in a county jail cell. People hold grave concerns of retaliation. Officials are wary of law enforcement being usurped by the mob. Feelings are so great against Herman's attacker that safeguards need to be taken all along the way to see that justice is served under the law, not outside it.

James Hulbert calms the crowd and organizes a search. Officers from Lawrenceburg, reinforced by officers and private citizens from various locations in Indiana and Ohio, are to scour the area looking for Anderson. They will search in the marsh between Dearborn County, Indiana and Harrison, Ohio. James Anderson was last employed as a farm hand at Brookville and some officers will look for him there. Most recently Anderson lived in Connersville. Officials there are already on the hunt.

~

A man—whom I heard identify himself as County Commissioner William Hornberger—meets Mom at the jail. He and the other commissioners, Leonard Harper and Harry Dean, offer a $500 reward for information leading to the arrest and conviction of Dad's shooter.

Mom spends the rest of the afternoon talking to a number of people, many of whom I didn't know. They talk about Dad's condition, the search for Anderson, the two men in the jail, and what they can do to help. Mom never waivers and talks to each and every one of them. I don't know how she does it. I am a wreck. I want to see Dad. Mom tells me maybe tomorrow.

After supper Mom leaves with Hulbert to see Dad at the hospital. I beg to go, but she demands that my job is school. I need to care for my studies and let her do the worrying. Aunt Dora stays with me. Lafe minds the jail for the night. I go to bed. I don't sleep. I have one eye open watching the door to the jail. It's not cold, but I shiver all the same. Mom returns late.

Early Tuesday Mom rushes me off to school again as she readies herself to return to Dad's side. I again beg to go but she says maybe later. I go grudgingly. Mom stops in her tracks and chides, "You can't stop a scared thought from coming into your head. But you don't need to pull up a chair and bid it sit down."

Right after lunch, Dora picks me up at school. I am excited to get to go, yet I am worried by the sight of her tear-stained face. Lafe is with her. I hop in his car for the ride to Cincinnati.

I arrive at the hospital, and Mom meets me in the lobby. She finds a place out of the way to sit and talk. She isn't crying but I sense the concern in her reddened eyes. There is no trace of any smile as she begins to talk. "Stella, late Monday after the surgery the doctors told me that Dad's wounds are serious and very well might prove to be fatal. There is little more they could do to help him. They could only try to care for his pain. This morning peritonitis set in."

Mom tries to explain what this is, but all I understand is that Dad's hours are numbered. His brother, Alpha is here now. Dad has only a short time to live.

Mom takes my hand and leads me upstairs to Dad's room. Entering the darkened room, my eyes squint to search his pale, pain-wearied face. His hair is mussed and the gown he wears is wrinkled with some dried stains of blood on the front. I am scared. I say nothing. I try to muster all the courage I have to fight back sobs caught in my throat. After a short while, Dad seems to paint a faint smile on his dry lips. He reaches up to pat my hair. I kiss his blanched brow. His smile wanes again and Mom ushers me out of the room. She puts her arm around me and hugs me and then passes me to Dora. I break down crying. Dora and I return to the waiting area where we sit. I stare blankly at the floor. My senses escape me. I sob and close my eyes as if in a dream. A flock of men in suits, carrying briefcases and legal pads hurry into Dad's room.

~

Prosecuting Attorney, Julius Schwing, and former judge, Charles Lowe, called Detective Ora Slater, former Dearborn County Sheriff and a boyhood friend of Herman's. Slater was called to take a statement from Herman at the hospital. This statement would be needed to prosecute Anderson when he was found. Herman was very weak but he mumbled the following statement to Ora Slater and his stenographer, Howard L. Shearer. Cincinnati, Ohio, December 31, 1929.

"I, Herman Lange, being now fully convinced that I am going to die from an injury sustained on the morning of December 30, 1929, when I was shot, and with the full realization of impending death certain from my present injuries, do hereby voluntarily make the following statement as to facts as to how I was shot."

"The man who did the shooting was James Anderson. He told me that was his name. He wore high top, lace shoes, blue

corduroy pants, black overcoat, and black hat. I went to Brookville and met the sheriff of Franklin County and on the road back I saw Anderson, and I went back and asked if he wanted a ride. I stopped and I got out of the car and the wind must have blown my coat back, and when he saw my badge, he shot." (Signed) Herman Lange[33]

Family at his side, Herman Thomas Lange ended his watch as Sheriff of Dearborn County, Indiana at ten p.m. on Tuesday, December 31, 1929. He died twelve hours shy of a year after taking his oath of office. Son, Brother, Husband, Father, farmer, bailiff, sheriff is now only a memory.

~

Head buried in her chest, Mom walks out of Dad's hospital room. I glance at the clock on the wall above the door. It reads 10:15 PM. I look back at Mom. She doesn't need to say a word. I know. Dad is dead.

---

[33] *The Lawrenceburg Press, 09 January 1930, 1*

9

"Funeral"

I am afraid. Dad died today. What will we do? Everyone offers us condolences. Their best wishes don't stop the hurt. Their hugs don't bring Dad back to us. I'm not going to school this week

Stella Mae Lange – *My Journal, 12/31/1929*

Three strange men in business suits show up at our front door this morning. It's New Year's Day. I thought everyone would let me and Mom alone today. Mom opens the door and welcomes them.

~

On Wednesday, January 1, 1930, the County Commissioners appointed Mayme Lange to complete her dead husband's term as Sheriff of Dearborn County. *The Lawrenceburg Register* recalls, *This is the first time in the county that a sheriff met death while in the performance of his duties. Historical records of the county show that Mrs. Lange, who has been appointed to fill the unexpired term of her deceased husband, will be the thirty-eighth sheriff to serve the county and the first woman to hold the office.*[34] Mayme is the first woman sheriff in the State of Indiana

Mayme Lange's Sheriff Badge

~

It is a holiday, but not for me. At the jail, Mom has her head buried in papers at the desk. I don't know what she is doing and don't care. Mom looks up from her papers to prepare me for what is coming. She tells me that Dad's dead body will shortly be brought home to our family residence at the jail? I lose control. My numbed mind will not awake until the entire funeral ordeal is over.

————————————————— ~

[34] *The Lawrenceburg Register, 09 January 1930, 1*

Herman Lange's body lays in state in the Court Room at the Dearborn County Courthouse on Friday, January 3, from one p.m. to five p.m. The Robert McAllister American Legion Post furnishes the honor guard at the courthouse. This is only the second time that such a tribute as this has been paid to an official of the county. Friends by the score file through the courthouse, passing by the casket to look upon his still face as a tribute of respect and appreciation of his exceptionally fine qualities as a courageous officer and a plain man of the people.

Flags throughout the county fly at half-mast to honor the humble hero. Likewise, a flag is draped across the fallen sheriff's coffin. The rolling red stripes of the flag suggest the blood that flowed from Herman's body. The sailcloth white canvas stripes of the flag hints at the purity of intention with which Sheriff Lange served. The bold blue field emblazoned with stars evokes soothing thoughts of the better place in which Herman now rests.

Funeral services are held at the Zion Lutheran Church in Manchester— founded by Herman's great-uncle Christian Busse—on Saturday, January 4, 1930. The funeral at the church is the largest such ceremony ever held there. Pall bearers are all Dearborn County officials. Burial is held at the Greendale Cemetery.

Herman is eulogized by his long-time friend and mentor, Judge Charles Lowe. Lowe had coaxed Herman into the public arena years earlier. The Sheriff had no regrets for his decision to follow the Judge's lead into the service of his fellow Hoosiers. The Judge sings praise to his friend's dedication, offers thanks for his tireless effort. With a lawyer's polished oratory, Charles' words for his dear friend settle into the hearts of all present at the church.

The Death Certificate lists the cause of death as peritonitis caused by gunshot wound to the abdomen. There was no autopsy done in Cincinnati's Bethesda Hospital. There was a post-mortem examination held on Thursday by Coroner C. C. Marshall at the Moon and Schopmeyer Funeral Home. This autopsy reveals that the bullet, a 38 caliber, entered the front of the abdomen, pierced the colon twice and then lodged in the back of the abdominal cavity close to the spinal column.

Herman Lange Death Certificate

Herman was a young man of 40 years when he died. He and his wife Mayme and their daughter Stella, had an eternity of promise before them. What was it that shattered that promise? Was it the failings of Indiana Agriculture? Was it the evil of Prohibition? Was it the despair fueled by the

Depression? Was it only the frightened reaction of a young man in trouble? Mayme and Stella would have a lifetime to question that promise, an eternity to answer the question.

~

I awoke the day after the funeral. The day falls before me, the same cruel length as it always is. Mom and I attend church services Sunday morning. I didn't cry today.

10

"Manhunt"

Dad's shooter is on the run. Mom says James Anderson will be captured soon. She is now sheriff and must know what is happening. I am still afraid. Who will keep the murderer from coming after Mom and me? I can't sleep.
Stella Mae Lange – My Journal, 01/04/1930

The funeral is over. Church is not a blessed event. Lots of people hug, offer sympathy, and try to comfort me. Mom stays close by me, but I see her being dragged from person to person as well. We make it through the gauntlet and head home for a quiet Sunday afternoon to pause and retreat from all that has happened. I even enjoy spending time doing some mindless math homework to escape talking or crying.

I know things won't remain quiet. Mom has James Hulbert and two county commissioners coming for dinner this evening. She now holds the office of sheriff. A lot of organizing faces her in getting the help she needs to police the county and to find Dad's murderer. She tells the dinner guests that she wants James Hulbert to be her deputy. He is a well-known, local businessman and a former Republican candidate for sheriff. He lost to Dad in the May 1928 Republican

Primary. The commissioners agree with the assignment and charge Hulbert to begin discharging his duties.

Housing Bradburn and Seiter, the killer's friends, in Mom's jail demands too much of her. Looking at these prisoners with unbiased eyes weighs heavy on Mom. Caring for these prisoners tasks Mom more than one could ask. She chokes back her tears and carries out her duty.

I miss Dad. I awake with a start at times—believing he is still here. The jail never seemed like home. Mom and Dad loved me, but here we were living in a fishbowl, always in the view of deputies, judges, prisoners. The jail occupies a world far removed from our dear, lovely farm. I dry my eyes and look out of the fishbowl at the flurry of activity around the jail. Living at the jailhouse and so near to the courthouse, I can't help but see what happens. I don't want to know, but I can't look away.

~

The shooting victim from "Spike's camp" Ben Shaw dies. Pressure to catch the shooter mounts. Law enforcement spins a web to trap the killer. Other hands are tugging at the threads that bind the ugly bootleg camps, unraveling the evil tapestry Prohibition and Depression have woven.

Mayme talks to Ora Slater, Cal Crim Detective from Cincinnati. Herman knew Ora from their days working at the Big Four Railroad. He offers to help find and capture James Anderson. His presence reassures. Mayme smiles when he is here. Slater's reputation advertises that he always gets his man. He knows the territory, and Mayme welcomes his help.

Officers and others from all around Indiana and Ohio

scour the area looking for James Anderson. Numerous reports of his location fail to uncover his whereabouts. Sheriff Leon Neal of Ohio County, Lafe Perpington, and Harry Hunter find Walter Anderson, the killer's 23 year-old brother, about eight miles north of Brookville at the farm of William Martin southwest of Blooming Grove. They immediately arrest, charge him with aiding a fugitive to escape, and bring him to the Lawrenceburg jail. They find Leonard Burch, Anderson's brother-in-law, at his place of employment, the Auburn automobile plant in Connersville. They likewise bring him to jail and hold both relatives to gain information about James Anderson.

The fugitive flees in Burch's automobile the day following the shooting of Sheriff Lange. James Anderson has a bad shoulder wound according to his brother Walter, even though the brother still denies knowledge of James' whereabouts. Sheriff Mayme Lange now has four friends, relatives, accompli of the shooter housed in her jail. Their presence forebodes a bad night's sleep. The notion that the killer's friends and relatives are housed in their home terrifies Mayme and Stella.

Posses from Lawrenceburg and Brookville scour the hills around Metamora and Laurel searching for the murder suspect. They believe Anderson to be in the area, yet they find no trace.

The Dearborn County Circuit Court appoints former Circuit Court Judge Charles Lowe to assist Prosecuting Attorney Julius Schwing—welcome good news for the Lange women. They know Judge Lowe has a personal interest in this journey to justice.

The court appoints George Goodpaster and Tom Owens as special bailiffs to clean up the notorious beer camps, to arrest the operators and padlock the places of illegal operation. Mayme believes the actions to clean up the speakeasies to be long overdue. People across the county harbor a lot of resentment for the evil the activities at these camps inflicted upon Herman.

Judge Ricketts orders a thorough investigation of violations at the camps along the Whitewater River. Special bailiffs Goodpaster and Owens feverishly attack their mission. On the evening of Monday, January 6, the pair padlock two camps near Harrison, "The Barn" and "Spike's". Next, on Wednesday morning, they padlock the Barber camp in Logan Township near New Trenton and the Meninger camp near the Harrison Bridge. They load a truck full of bottles, slot machines, glasses, cans, and much more evidence and take it to the jail.

Judge Ricketts deals swift justice to those bootleggers brought before him. Adam "Spike" Knosp pleads guilty. The judge sentences him to four months on the penal farm and a fine of $200. Fred Schwing, who operated a soft drink stand near the Harrison Bridge, pleads guilty to a liquor charge and receives a sentence of three months on the penal farm and a fine of $200. Charles "Charcoal" Smith pleads guilty and gets a sentence of thirty days on the penal farm and a fine of $150. Mrs. Etta Klingelhoffer pleads guilty and gets a sentence of thirty days in the county jail and fine of $200. Frank Barber pleads guilty and receives a sentence of three months on the penal farm and a fine of $200. George Meninger pleads not guilty and will be tried later. The court orders the places liquor was sold to be padlocked for one year. Where were these actions when the Sheriff was alive?

Concern for Herman's death drives law enforcement's

activity against the bootleg camps across Dearborn's borders. Neighboring Indiana County and Federal agencies heighten attacks on the evils of Prohibition. The front page of *The Brookville Democrat* talks about liquor raids staged in Franklin County under the direction of federal officers. This is right in Mayme's backyard.

Nine citizens of Brookville, one from Laurel and another from New Trenton were caught in a liquor raid which was staged in this county last Friday afternoon. The raid was led by J. E. Wilkey, deputy prohibition enforcement officer of Indiana assisted by seven federal agents.

Charges of sale and possession were filed. All charges of sale were made on government "buys" by an under-cover agent, who has been in Brookville the past six or seven weeks.

The visit to this county by the federal agents was quite unexpected, the local officials having no knowledge in advance of the raid.[35]

A frenzy of activity produces a remedy for the plague of illegal bootlegging operations as the search for the killer continues to bear no fruit. Although under arrest, Walter Anderson and Leonard Burch, relatives of the killer, prove to be less than helpful to officials. Mayme and Stella cringe watching them sit in the jail refusing to offer information of Herman's killer. Finally, continued and severe grilling of the duo provides a lead to Anderson's possible location—family in southeastern Kentucky in Harlan County. He might go there to be with his father.

On Monday, January 6, Leon Neal, Harry Hunter, Glenn Bryant, Otis Roehm, and Lewis Wilson travel to Livingston, Kentucky hoping to interview Anderson's father. Detective Ora

[35] *The Brookville Democrat, 06 March 1930, 1*

Slater aids in the investigation. They hope this will secure information leading to the killer's arrest.

When the officers arrive in Livingston, they are unable to locate Anderson's father. He receives a tip that they are coming and flees the area. The search for the killer dead ends. It angers many that the hills can hide a killer like that.

J. R. Williams' editorial in *The Lawrenceburg Press* sums the area's feelings. *An awakened public conscience throughout Dearborn County is asserting itself on all sides over the outrageous murder of Sheriff Herman Lange and the causes and incidents leading thereto. This courageous peace officer and fine gentleman was foully shot down by a lawless and brutal vagabond, a fugitive from justice, on the highway...near a beer camp on Whitewater river not far from Harrison, Ohio, Monday morning of last week, dying Tuesday evening. All circumstances go to show that the man, James Anderson, charged with this heinous crime, was as if lying in ambush to assassinate Sheriff Lange, as he knew the officer would be in search of him for previously shooting and fatally wounding another man the same night. This reckless bravado and assassin after committing these foul crimes, resulting in dual murder, made his escape and up to Wednesday had not been captured, despite the fact that officers are scouring the country in their efforts to capture him that he may be made to pay the penalty.*

Feeling has been at a high pitch, reason almost dethroned, and it makes one shudder to think what retaliatory action in summary punishment might have taken place, had this villainous criminal been captured. But greater calmness now pervades the people and the sentiment is to continue the man hunt until the perpetrator is captured, then speedily invoke the law's decree in dealing out justice by and through the courts without unnecessary delay or hindrance.

His Honor, Judge William D. Ricketts, in convening Circuit Court Lawrenceburg, Monday morning, instructing the grand jury, dwelt especially upon this double murder and the disgraceful and unlawful conditions existing within the confines of Dearborn County in this beer camp on Whitewater River. He described it as a veritable hell hole, reeking in vice, debauchery and lawlessness of a revolting nature. He told the grand jurors that they must use every means at their command to root out and put an estoppel to this nefarious and lawless business and conduct. He told them they were empowered to summon before them whomsoever they might desire to aid them in ferreting out the guilty and bring indictments against them. He advised that frequenters at these camps, men and women, be brought before the jury, and if they failed in true testimony to indict them for libel. He declared that this place of iniquity and sin must be broken up and those responsible for its existence driven out and punished.

The grand jury is now diligently at work to investigate this camp situation and its relation to this awful; tragedy which cost the lives of Sheriff Lange and a Mr. Shaw, the latter unfortunately being a patron of one of the camps, while the officer was slain in discharge of his duties.

Judge Ricketts is being widely commended by the public for his vigorous charge and his bold stand to drive from the confines of Dearborn County and other counties in this judicial district, vicious criminal institutions, such as those at this beer camp, which are reported to have been running wide open for some time. His Honor likewise calls upon the citizenship of Dearborn and other counties to be outspoken and stand firm for strict law enforcement to the end that safety to life and property and better conditions socially and industrially may exist.

Public sentiment has much to do with all matters of law and life, hence every individual has or should have a self-imposed duty to meet in upholding the laws of our land. It is too bad, however, that a foul murder, such as befell Sheriff Lange, ,must take place before a check is placed against causes or means to prevent similar recurrences.

To your tents, Oh Israel! Countrymen, be men of courage, candor and honor, and give aid to the courts and officials in their warfare against lawlessness and particularly against that which leads to murder and degradation of character. In that way can the life of Sheriff Lange be avenged, and it can likewise be said that he did not die in vain. [36]

~

The search for justice begins. Mom and I can only pray they find Dad's murderer soon.

---

[36] J. R. Williams, *The Lawrenceburg Press, Editorial,* 09 January 1930

11

"Killer Captured"

It's been weeks and still no hope of finding James Anderson. I can't believe Mom and I will always fear this killer showing up at our door step. With every prisoner entering our house, I wonder if he is the one who took my Father from us.

Stella Mae Lange - My *Journal, 03/01/1930*

I'm going to the basketball game tonight. Lawrenceburg plays Aurora. Some of the kids at school say it will be great to beat Aurora as they were the sectional champs last year. I don't know about that. I'm just looking forward to seeing my old friends, especially Ginny. We'll have a super time, and I really need to get out of the house.

Mom thinks I should stay home. She may be all wrapped up in the search for Dad's murderer, but I need to get out and get away. I know Mom's upset that James Anderson has not been caught yet. I am too, but he hides way down in Kentucky and far from us.

Having said her piece, Mom finally agrees to let me go to the game. You better believe I'm out the door before she changes her mind. Mom walks me the three blocks to the high school. I see Ginny outside the gym and I am off and running.

~

Mayme knows they're hot on James Anderson's trail. He is the object of one of the most intensive manhunts in the history of Dearborn and Franklin counties. Posses of deputies, police, and citizens scour the countryside looking for him. He manages to elude capture by searchers on several occasions escaping them by mere minutes.

More than two months of following leads, interviewing Anderson's relatives, friends, and neighbors, consulting with local Kentucky law enforcement produce little glimmer of hope that the killer would be found. Mayme will not allow herself to be disheartened. Prosecutor Julius Schwing, Assistant Prosecutor Judge Charles Lowe, and Circuit Court Judge William Ricketts call upon Ora Slater—due to his dogged determination in pursuit of criminals—to assist in the apprehension of Anderson. Mayme says that Slater knows how to capture criminals.

Slater and Hulbert go to various locations in Kentucky on a number of occasions to find Anderson or information about his whereabouts. They follow leads to Livingston, Mount Vernon, Hazel Patch, London, and Hazard, Kentucky. These towns in the hills of south-central Kentucky are protective of their people both by the geography of tough mountainous terrain and the temperament of tough mountain people. Mayme likens them to Hoosiers living in the hills.

~

I think Lawrenceburg won, but I don't care. I have a great time. Ginny introduces me to a couple of boys she knows, but they are more interested in the game. We lose them and find a spot under the bleachers where we can catch up on our lost time.

Saturday morning at breakfast, I am excited to tell Mom all the news from Ginny at the game the night before. Mom's head hears a different drum—not our conversation. She says things are moving quickly with Anderson's capture and she may need to leave if things start to happen. I bite my lip and slouch back in my chair. Mom offers her news anyway, "Perry County, Kentucky, Sheriff Gross, finally arrested and held Anderson near Hazard. The arrest was made upon information obtained by former Sheriff W. M. Cornett of Perry County. The sheriff said that Anderson admitted shooting Sheriff Lange, but contended that he fired only after the sheriff shot him in the shoulder and the back of the head." She stops her story right there. She tightens her fist and growls, "That's not how it happened."

Mom remains quiet the rest of the day. Her face is a knot of anger, but her gray eyes seem to come from somewhere else, two pools of expectation. She does a little paperwork, talks to one of the deputies, and finishes some of her bookkeeping. She looks busy, but I can tell her mind wanders. Her attention lives in Kentucky, not Lawrenceburg for the next couple of days. Her anxious wait may end soon.

~

On Tuesday, March 11, 1930, James Anderson, wanted for Herman's murder, is finally captured. A 72 day search ends. All the resources of Dearborn County's law enforcement and judicial organization bear the burden of finding and convicting the murderer of their beloved sheriff. They find James Anderson. Justice will be served.

Both area newspapers deliver the same account of Anderson's capture. *The Lawrenceburg Press* and *The Lawrenceburg Register* tell the story of the murderer's arrest Tuesday.

The following statement of the apprehension of Anderson was given to the Register (also Press) by Detective Ora Slater of Cincinnati and Deputy Hulbert of Lawrenceburg.

On New Year's Eve Prosecutor Julius Schwing and Assistant Prosecutor Judge Charles *A. Lowe called Detective Ora Slater to the Bethesda Hospital, Cincinnati, as a witness to take Sheriff Herman Lange's dying statement. In that statement the Sheriff said that James Anderson shot him on the road near Longenecker's Station. Lange also stated that the man who shot him told him his name was James Anderson. The Sheriff stated that when he stepped from his car the wind blew his coat back and Anderson saw his badge.*

Later in a conference with Judge Ricketts, Prosecutor Schwing and Assistant Prosecutor Lowe, Slater was asked to assist in the apprehension of Anderson. Slater and Deputy Sheriff Hulbert then went to Mount Vernon, the county seat of Rock Castle County, Kentucky, where Sheriff Tipton is well acquainted with the Andersons. Tipton advised Slater and Deputy Sheriff Hulbert to get away from there as soon as possible, so as not to arouse suspicion and that the posse that had come down there previously had caused considerable excitement at Livingston, which is ten miles from Mount Vernon. On this trip Deputy Sheriff Hulbert had a warrant in his possession for James Anderson, charging him with first degree murder. This warrant he left with Sheriff Tipton, who stated that he would do all in his power to apprehend Anderson and would immediately notify the Sheriff's office at Lawrenceburg when he did. Hazel Patch, where Anderson formerly resided, is in Rock Castle County, and Sheriff Tipton advised them to go to London, Kentucky. And confer with Sheriff Steele at that place, as Anderson had relatives in that County. Slater and Hulbert immediately went there and Sheriff Steele advised them to go back home at once, so as not to arouse any suspicion. They took his advice and returned.

Later Sheriff Steele called Slater at Cincinnati to come down and confer with relatives of Anderson as they were to be in his office the next day. Acting under instructions of the Prosecutor of Dearborn county Slater went to London, Kentucky and Jones Durham, an uncle of Anderson, and another uncle named Robinson were in the Sheriff's office. Both stated that they did not know where Jim was, but if the Prosecutor would turn Walter Anderson loose, who was being held in jail at Lawrenceburg, they might turn James over to Sheriff Steele or the authorities at Lawrenceburg if he could be given a life sentence. They later tried to make a deal whereby if Jim was turned over, tried and convicted, that the Prosecutor recommend leniency, which offer was refused. They then came to Lawrenceburg and talked with the Prosecutor and Judge in an effort to arrange to turn James over, to take a plea of guilty and be sentenced for life. During this time James had been hidden in one of the three counties, Rock Castle, Laurel or Breathitt. Last reports were that they were waiting for excitement to die down before they made another move. Owing to the location of houses where Anderson lived, it was a hard matter to approach without being detected and it was not deemed advisable to not comply with the requests of the Sheriff's there, as they stated they would apprehend Anderson soon as they could locate him.

Walter Anderson had stated that he had driven his brother, James, to DeCourcy, Kentucky, after the shooting, which was false, as it has been proven that he drove him all the way down to the vicinity of Hazel Patch, as the mileage indicated on the car that they used on the trip.

The Prosecutor's office has been in constant touch with Sheriffs in the different counties where Anderson might be located and received word several days ago that they might expect good news soon.

On the morning of Tuesday, March 11, Anderson was arrested by Perry County, Kentucky, authorities at Buckhorn, Kentucky, about twenty-five miles from Hazard. The arrest was made by Deputies Alfred Amis and Sam Begley. Anderson was staying at the home of a relative in the hill country. When the officers called at the home Anderson ran out but was captured after a short chase. He did not have a gun on his person, but one was found in the house. This fact was verified by a phone call from Detective Slater to the Sheriff at Hazard, when he stated they were bringing him to turn over to Dearborn County authorities. He will be placed in another jail other than Dearborn County's jail.

A statement that Mr. Slater wishes to make is that in his many years of criminal investigation, he never knew officers to work harder than the officials who worked here. And the only way to get results where a man is hiding out like Anderson was, is to comply with the requests made by the authorities in other counties in order not to cause friction.

Sheriff Leon Neal of Rising Sun has also worked with

Deputy Sheriff Hulbert and made a trip with him through Kentucky in an effort to assist the authorities there in apprehending Anderson. It has been a case of team work with the authorities here and those in Kentucky which has resulted in Anderson's apprehension.

Detective Slater made many extra trips to Kentucky without any charge... Slater did this out of love and loyalty to his home county.[37]

~

The big old clock hanging above Mom's desk clangs eight dongs. The calendar proclaims Wednesday, March 12. Mom fails to warn me what is about to happen. A flurry of activity stirs in our home. There are people all over, many whom I do not know. All heck breaks loose as a couple of strange men in ill-fitting suits drag a dirty, scruffy, wild-eyed, shackled young man into the jail office. Through the grime-covered hair hanging in his eyes, he appears to be not much older than me. He smells like a field of crushed, rotting November corn stalks. I peek from behind the doorway as they bring the man into the jail office. His dark eyes look straight into mine. Even the wood-stove in the corner cannot warm the chill crawling up my spine. Chains restrain him, but I am still scared. My heart sinks and I turn and rush out of the room to catch my breath.

Mom appears strangely unsettled as she tugs at her glasses. Hands shaking, she reaches for her large bound sheriff arrest log. There are a number of men in my way, but I can glance around the corner and see Mom as she speaks. "Who is this prisoner, Deputy Hulbert?"

---

[37] *The Lawrenceburg Press,* 13 March 1930, 1

The deputy answers, "This is James Anderson, ma'am. He's been brought here from Hazard by Kentucky officials, W. A. Cornett and Sam Bagley. He is under indictment for the murder of Dearborn County Sheriff Herman Thomas Lange. He's to be held here at the jail in Lawrenceburg until trial arrangements can be made."

My mouth drops. I shudder. My knees tremble. I sit down.

Mom steadies her nerves and enters Anderson's information in the arrest log. As she writes, I can see through the front door a crowd gathering in the street outside our home. Mom also notices the crowd. With Anderson locked in his cell, Hulbert leaves the room with Mom and a couple of the men. Concerns for the safety of the captured James Anderson are cause for Mom and the others to find a venue other than Lawrenceburg to house the accused murderer. I draw a relieved breath hearing that this man will not be in our jail, our home, very long.

~

The decision to move Anderson out of the jail unfolds in the following order by Judge Ricketts. *The above named James Anderson has been indicted by the Grand Jury of Dearborn County, Indiana, and charged with the murder of Herman Lange, which murder was alleged to have occurred on the 30th day of December, 1929, and James Anderson has been apprehended and is now in the custody of officials of the Commonwealth of Kentucky, and it being shown to the court that there might be a possibility of violence being done to the said James Anderson, if he were brought at this time to*

Dearborn County, Indiana.

It is now by the court ordered that the said James Anderson, be confined in the County Jail of Decatur County, at Greensburg, Indiana, pending the hearing of said cause in the Dearborn County Circuit Court or until the further order of this court herein, and is now ordered that a copy of this order be delivered and turned over to the Sheriff of Decatur County, Indiana, and the same shall be sufficient authority for him to confine the said James Anderson under said charge.[38]

~

I cannot sleep. I see the shadowy silhouettes of two men leading the shackled Anderson out of the jail around midnight. Mom moves with them through the office and into the night air. I hear them say that Deputy Hulbert and Dr. J. M. Jackson of Aurora are taking the prisoner to the Ripley County Jail in Versailles. They will then move Anderson up State Route 46 to the Greensburg Jail in Decatur County on Thursday evening, March 13.

~

Things at the jail calm down a little with Anderson housed elsewhere. While in Greensburg, James Anderson reportedly becomes intensely religious. Anderson attests to his new religious fervor and his desire to get right with God as his reason to surrender. Perhaps he had forgotten that the paper

---

[38] *State of Indiana vs. James Anderson, No. 3603,* Dearborn County Circuit Court, 12 March 1930

said he ran when officials tried to arrest him at a relative's house in Hazard a week earlier. Decatur County officials are so taken by Anderson's religious facade they accompany him to church services in Greensburg on Sunday, March 16. Succumbing to tears launched by the murderer's account of his crimes, the entire congregation of the First Baptist Church breaks into a solemn "Bringing in the Sheaths." Anderson begs to be baptized. He confesses his sins. Reverend J. P. Mitchell baptizes the killer. Herman's murderer says he is willing to die for the slayings. He adds that if he receives a life sentence, he will devote his entire prison life to the Lord's work. One wonders if his religious experience is real or a ploy to sway the press in attendance at the church.

The Dearborn County Circuit Court will convene next Monday, March 24. Anderson's case is to be reviewed then. The prisoner's new religious attitude causes officials to presume that he will plead guilty. As Anderson now offers to confess, people believe he will place himself at the mercy of the Court. This portends to be an important piece in solving the conviction puzzle.

The *Brookville Democrat's* March 13, front page article of James Anderson's capture *is* the only source in Franklin, Ohio, or Dearborn counties to offer the possibility of a plea of self-defense.

Anderson's story of the shooting differs from the deathbed statement made by Sheriff Lange to Prosecutor Julius Schwing and Assistant Prosecutor Charles Lowe, Dearborn County, in the Bethesda Hospital, New Year's Eve according to Ora Slater operative of the Cal Crim Detective Bureau. Slater was called into the case by Prosecutor Schwing and was one of those present when Sheriff Lange made his dying statement.

"The sheriff stated that he did not know Anderson when he gave him a 'lift' in his automobile." Slater said "Lange said that the man told him that his name was 'Jim Anderson', but Lange did not know that he was wanted in connection with the beer camp shooting. Lange said that as they were riding along the wind blew back the lapel of his coat and that when Anderson saw his badge he pulled out his revolver and shot the sheriff."

Slater said that the sheriff denied having fired the first shot.[39]

~

The story worries Mom. She hopes that they get a confession that sticks. She can't imagine James Anderson getting released.

---

[39] *The Brookville Democrat,* 13 March 1930, 1

12

"Confession"

Mom says James Anderson confessed to killing Dad. We all knew that he was guilty. Mom says that the confession will bring the ordeal to a swift conclusion. With his admission of guilt he will have a quick and decisive trial. We will get our lives back. We will have to live in fear no more.

Stella Mae Lange – *My Journal, 03/16/1930*

Lawrenceburg played basketball against Milan last night. Ginny and I went. I needed to get away. There's been way too much going on at home. All sorts of people are in and out of Mom's office at the jail. I would like to just take it easy and sleep in this morning. The phone rings around 6:30 a.m. and ruins that good idea for me. Mom answers the phone. I wake to see what holds her attention. Mom says the Decatur County Sheriff called saying James Anderson wants to make a voluntary signed confession.

This development excites Mom. She believes this will seal the deal of Anderson getting what he deserves. This afternoon Deputy Sheriff James Hulbert, Prosecutor Julius C. Schwing, Assistant Prosecutor Judge Charles A. Lowe, and Detective Ora Slater will head north to meet Decatur County

Sheriff Newt Coy. These men will question Anderson and take his voluntary statement. This group scares me. I am certain they will intimidate James Anderson. I agree with Mom. This ordeal appears to be almost over. It has been 76 days since Dad's murder. Dearborn County officials will have a rock solid case to bring justice.

I'm staying home tonight. This morning the phone was a nuisance. Tonight the phone should bring Mom and me good news. I want to be around when Mom gets the call.

Late, around 7:00 p.m., Mom calls me to dinner. We're having beef stew that Aunt Dora brought over just a few minutes ago. Friends and relatives have been helping Mom out with cooking quite a bit lately. I like Dora's cooking, but my busy mind forgets to tell my mouth to eat. Mom's quiet and I nibble at the beef chunks on the plate before me. Mom jumps as the phone rings. She hurries to her desk to answer this call. I can tell by the pitch of her voice that this must be good news. She thanks the caller and returns to the table. "Good news," she exclaims. "We have a guilty man's confession."

I am all ears as Mom tells me of the day's events in Greensburg. Prosecutors Schwing and Lowe advised Anderson of his right to legal representation. They explained to him that he was not being called upon or in any way urged to make a statement, as what he might say would be used against him in court. They were covering all of their bases. They were determined that the long wait for their chance to bring your Father's killer to justice would not be wasted. Ora Slater delivered the needed admissions from James Anderson. Mom wiped a tear from the corner of her eye as she sighed, "We are almost done. We needed this to happen."

~

Ora Slater took the dying statement of Herman Lange. Ora Slater was brought in to question Walter Anderson, the killer's brother, about the whereabouts of James Anderson. Ora Slater went to Livingston, Kentucky, to find and question James Anderson's father about hiding the killer. Who is Ora Slater?

Ora Major Slater was born in Lawrenceburg in 1874. He was grandson of Richard Dawes Slater, who had served in both the Indiana House and Senate. His father, Jasper served as a deputy sheriff in Dearborn County, setting a heroic example for his son. Ora followed in his father's footsteps. He was elected to two terms as sheriff of Dearborn County.

It is early in the investigation and manhunt of James Anderson and already Ora Slater is taking a vital role. In the late 1920's local law enforcement agencies, even large metropolitan ones like Cincinnati, did not have professional investigative detective organizations within their scope of capability. Search for criminals and clues leading to arrest and conviction were something that an agency would often have to contract to a private investigative firm.

Cal Crim, Inc. was founded in 1913 by David Calvin Crim, retired Chief of Detectives for Cincinnati Police Department, and Ora Slater. In the early years there were no FBI or state crime units and it was not unusual for a city, county or even state government to retain the services of Cal Crim or his associates to conduct criminal investigations which they considered to be beyond the capabilities of their local police departments.

Eugene Block's 1967 non-fiction account of *Famous Detectives: True Stories of Great Crime Detection* describes

Slater's investigative prowess. Chapter 11 of Block's book tells of "OHIO'S ACE INVESTIGATOR, *Ora E. Slater*". One of the stories about Slater deals with his work on a murder case in Canton, Ohio in July, 1926. Don Mellett, the editor and publisher of the *Canton Daily News*, was known for his fearless attacks on underworld corruption and his charges of police collusion in bootleg activities. On a late night return home from dinner with his wife, Mellett was murdered with two shots to the head. There seemed to be clear motive for the killing but no one believed the police would ever bring the murderer to justice.

The following text from Block's *Famous Detectives* offers a glimpse into the understanding of Slater's ability. *Slater, the publishers knew, was recognized as one of the ablest, shrewdest detectives in the country, a human dynamo whose lack of formal education was more than balanced by his lightning brain, keen insight and amazing memory. He was credited with an uncanny way of "looking through people," quickly judging their character; and of knowing just how to bore into puzzling cases to ferret out the truth. On occasion, in vital interrogations, he bluffed but he knew just when and how to do it. Rarely did such a strategy fail.*

He could recall minor details of events long passed. Some said that he could "smell a crook" from a distance. His memory for faces was surprising. Once he hailed by name a passerby on a Cincinnati street -- a man he had met for only a few minutes five years before in a prison yard.

He understood human values and knew just when to be tough or to appear soft and sympathetic -- an ability he once demonstrated when he was on the staff of the Indiana Reformatory. A supposedly "hardened" prisoner had defied all efforts to obtain a confession to a series of robberies. Slater begged for a chance to try.

First smoking with the man, Slater quickly found that behind a gruff exterior lay a sensitive, sentimental vein. He talked to the prisoner of various things -- life, death and home. The conversation was resumed the following day and Slater turned it to family ties. Suddenly a band outside struck up the strains of "Home, Sweet, Home." The prisoner broke into sobs and confessed. Slater than walked outside and paid the bandmaster he had hired for ten minutes. "Sugar captures more crooks than vinegar," Slater commented.[40]

As Block's words would attest, Ora Slater's persuasive familial manner would be the irritant lodged in Anderson's mind that produced the pearl that was his confession. This jewel will hopefully define the solid beauty of the case to be made for the Anderson's conviction.

~

Mom was ever so pleased that Ora Slater was the person to deliver Anderson's confession. It seems fitting for one Hoosier to care for another.

~

Anderson surprised the officials. He told them that his statement was meant to lift a burden from his heart. The confession was a means to get right with God. To be saved he would give the statement of his own volition.

---

[40] *Eugene* B. Block, *Famous Detectives, True Stories of Great Crime Detectives,* (Doubleday & Company, Inc., 1967), 209, 210, 211

On Monday evening March 17, The *Cincinnati Times-Star* offers Detective Ora Slater's take on Anderson's confession and its effect on the case.

The confession, said Slater, corroborated the dying statement of Sheriff Lange that Anderson had shot him before the sheriff fired at Anderson. "Anderson told us," said Slater, "that he had gotten religion and wanted to tell a story that was true. He said that he had fired several shots through the door of the camp near Harrison, one of which caused the death of Shaw, but he did not know it at the time."

"He said that he fired at Sheriff Lange when the sheriff ordered him to raise his hands and that the sheriff then returned the fire. Anderson also told about staying with relatives in Hazelpatch, Kentucky, for ten days in which his father had a doctor treat his wound." [41]

The following report from the March 20, 1930, *Lawrenceburg Register*, relates the confession with details of the entire story. The story begins as *he left the Estridge home in Franklin County on Sunday evening, December 28, in company with his two companions, Roscoe Bradburn and Gus Seiter. It continues until his arrest in Perry County, Kentucky, on Tuesday morning, March 11.*

He related how Bradburn and Seiter came to the Estridge home and asked him to accompany them that night. When Anderson asked where, the two replied, "You will find that out later." Liquor was passed around, all three taking a drink, after which they stayed a short while and then departed in a machine for Brookville. Before leaving the home Anderson obtained his gun and placed it on his person.

When they arrived at Brookville they went to a garage

---

[41] *The Cincinnati Times-Star*, 17 March 1930, 1

and bought some more whiskey. After remaining at this place a short time they left and went to another place operated by a man named Tom, where Bradburn bought still more liquor. Leaving there they went to Seiter's home, stayed a short time and went up to Brookville and drove around town for a short time.

When driving around in Brookville either Bradburn or Seiter proposed going to a camp along the river south of town. A stop was made at either Cedar Grove or New Trenton, where Anderson purchased some gasoline, cigarettes and chewing gum. The three then went on down the road, passing through Harrison and when they got to a camp near the Harrison Bridge, a stop was made and Bradburn bought more whiskey, Anderson paying for it. From here they went to the place known as "The Barn".

After arriving here, Anderson told of how Bradburn engaged in an argument with another man, a stranger to them, and how he and Seiter tried to quiet the two.

Finally the dance broke up and Anderson and his two companions left in their car and when they came to "Spike's" camp Bradburn proposed stopping. Anderson objected, saying there would be trouble and someone would get hurt. Bradburn had his way, went in and in a short time Anderson and Seiter followed.

Once in "Spike's" place the argument was renewed and Bradburn asked Anderson for his gun. Anderson at first refused but after Bradburn insisted that he have it, he turned the weapon over to Bradburn who flourished it in the crowd and later put it in his belt. A man, who it is said was "Spike" then slipped the gun away and unloaded it.

When the three were starting to go home "Spike" gave

the pistol to Anderson, who also asked for his cartridges. As the three were leaving the camp Anderson loaded the gun and when on the first step on the outside, fired three times through the door, then missed his step and fell in the road.

Anderson parted from his companions and started up the road, a car passing him which he denied shooting. Going a short distance he landed in a ditch, where he slept until he sobered up.

After awaking he struck a match to find his gun and hat and started on his way home. As to what transpired when he met Sheriff Lange he relates in his own language as follows:

"As I went out I noticed a fellow coming behind me, and when I hit the steps I turned and fired the pistol three times through the door and started away. Bradburn said wait a minute. I said no and started up the road. As a machine passed by I got too close to the roadside and fell over the embankment and lay there for some time. I don't know how long, naturally a man drunk, time will pass without his knowing. When I woke up I felt for my pistol and 'twas gone, examined my pocket book and it was empty. I struck a match and found my gun nearby. I got up and started home on the highway. Directly up rolls a machine and passed by twenty or thirty steps then stops. The driver stuck his head out and asked "Do you want a lift?" I said "I would not mind it", so I walked on up and as I got up near the car he said, "how far are you going?" and I said, "Brookville," so I walked around that way and laid my hand on the door and he must have come around that way, he said, "I will give you a lift" just like that, and I turned around and he said "what is your name", I said, "Anderson, is my name", he said "Uh, uh", and as he said "Uh, uh". He asked me where I was going, he said, "Where are you goin". I said,

"been going up the pike", he said, "what is your name", I said, "Anderson", and when I said Anderson, he flashed a light on me and I had on a hat and under the hat I saw the barrel of his gun in his right hand, he said, "your hands up". I did not throw them up, naturally a man that was in sin and under no God, when they come at him he will jerk for his gun and I jerked my pistol and fired at him and turned and as I turned around he fired and hit me in the shoulder and fired again and the other shot did not hit me. I walked around the end of the car and across the road and railroad and across the pike and on to the railroad and up the railroad a piece and back across the pike and into the field and went on through the fields."[42]

Anderson's quotes—found in *The Lawrenceburg Press*—answer the why of shooting both Shaw and Herman, *Anderson says he did not see Sheriff Lange's badge, nor did he know who he was until told later by some of his friends.*

He states that he never knew Shaw, who was killed at the camp and had not seen him until that night. Asked why he shot back through the door, "Because I was angry and intoxicated".

Anderson said it was still dark when the shooting (of Lange) took place. When asked if Lange said to him, "you are under arrest", He answered. "Positively no." [43]

In *The Lawrenceburg Register* Anderson continues his story of the events following his shooting along the road.

Finally he arrived at the home of Owen Estridge in Franklin County where he asked for a drink and informed the Estridges that he was shot. He then went to the home of Lloyd Estridge, where he took off coat and hat, put them in a suit

[42] *The Lawrenceburg Register,* 20 March 1930, 1
[43] *The Lawrenceburg Press,* 20 March 1930, 1

case and put on another coat and hat. He then went to the barn and remained there until Lloyd Estridge came home, when he asked him if Seiter and Bradburn had gotten in. Lloyd Estridge then informed Anderson that he had shot the sheriff of Dearborn County and a man by the name of Shaw, and that gangs of men were hunting him. Later Lloyd Estridge brought him his supper at the barn. Anderson then asked Estridge if he could get word to his brother, Walter Anderson, or to Leonard Burch. Lloyd told him no and went to the house, while Anderson remained in the loft of the barn.

After he had been in the loft a short time a man by the name of John Ebersole and Henry Estridge came to the barn and shouted for him. They asked if he was injured and if he was weak.

After this the two men took Anderson to the home of Henry Estridge where he told his (James Anderson) brother, Walter, about the shooting. From here Anderson was taken to the home of Leonard Burch at Connersville, by his brother Walter Anderson. Here Jim told his sister, Grace Burch, that he was shot and in trouble. Walter then asked Leonard Burch for his machine and Leonard informed him that he could not let him have it under the circumstances, but if he took it he could not help it.

Walter then took the car and he and James started for Kentucky, going through Alpine, Fairfield, thence to Hamilton and through Cincinnati, where they crossed into Kentucky. After crossing into Kentucky they stopped for dinner at a place called Fillmore's camp. Leaving here they proceeded on to Anderson's home near Hazelpatch. Here he told his father about his wound and the latter obtained a doctor, who gave him medical treatment. After this Anderson went to the home of an uncle where he stayed seven or eight days and then returned for a part of a day to his father's home, after which he was captured on March 11.

Anderson said that he left his gun with Henry Estridge, who gave it to Anderson's father and that the father had it the last time he saw it. He also said that his brother, Walter, left him at Parkers Creek, Kentucky.[44]

~

Just like Mom says, there appears to be a solid case against Anderson. He has confessed to shooting a man on the road after he had left the camp where he had shot through the door. Dearborn County Prosecutors have a death bed statement from Dad naming Anderson as the man who shot him. Mom wonders how solid?

Will justice be served? She fears a discrepancy exists between the statements of the two men regarding the shooting. Anderson's statement says that he did not recognize Dad, and that Dad had his gun pulled and then shot.

Dad's dying statement says that the wind blew his coat open revealing his gun and his badge. Upon seeing this, Anderson drew his gun and shot Dad first.

Mom remembers pleading with Dad to stop long enough so she could mend his loose coat button. He would not wait. I grabbed to hug him and the button fell. According to Mom, the fact that Dad's bullet wound is two inches below his badge indicates the shooter saw and aimed at the badge— adding credence to this account. There was no bullet hole in Dad's coat. This verifies that the coat was open when the bullet struck

[44] *The Lawrenceburg Register,* 20 March 1930, 1

114

the victim. Mom wonders how the differences in these accounts will affect Dearborn County's desire to impugn their beloved sheriff's killer.

I am thrilled that so much of this mess seems to be behind us. I am ready to be done with it all.

13

"Indiana's First Woman Sheriff "

*Mom won't run for sheriff. She knows I hate the constant fear
that she will be snatched from me just as Dad was. I dread the
thought of losing her too .Why can't everything just return to
being simple and easy. I miss the days on the farm. I miss Dad.*
Stella Mae Lange – *My Journal, 03/20/1930*

Things settle down a little now that James Anderson
confessed. I'm busy at school. We've got a play coming
up in April and I'm singing in the chorus. Mom's taking care
of the daily business of running the jail. James Anderson sits
behind bars in Greensburg. It's probably a good two months
before the trial. Mom wants me to get my head back into my
school work. I guess everything is about as normal as it's going
to get.

Mom has very little time for me lately. Sheriff duties bog
her down. As Matron of the jail while Dad was alive, she
cooked for prisoners and kept a ledger of expenses for
prisoners' meals. She kept a record of all mileage and other
expenses incurred by the sheriff's office. She now has someone
doing the cooking, but she records all the expenses and even
goes out on arrests.

Appointed by the County Commissioners as Dad's successor, Mom prides herself in being the first woman sheriff in Indiana. No one in Dearborn County seems to question her ability to serve as sheriff. Mom always stands tall and confident. I am amazed that she seldom seems to be overcome by the swirl of activity and people surrounding her. It bothers me and I'm not the one in charge. As sheriff, Mom never carries a gun. I can't recall ever seeing her handle a gun in all my years. I've overheard Deputy Hulbert whisper to others comparing Mom to Detective Ora Slater, who never used a gun in his dealings with 'bad' guys. However, Mom never goes out after someone without a deputy to accompany her.

Mom tries to go out on business while I am in school. Often, as I sit at the dining room table doing homework, Mom returns from an arrest and allows me to enter the information in the Sheriff's Log Book. I do notice a pattern in the types of problems she attacks. I see in the log book her name assigned to all types of domestic issues in the county. She makes arrests for intoxication, assault and battery, juvenile delinquency, failure to provide, and runaways. Intoxication and failure to provide arrests appear to be at the top of her lists. The evils surrounding Prohibition and the need to provide for the family weigh heavily influencing Mom's attention to the domestic issues of her job as sheriff.

With everything circling around her, Mom still takes the time to consider our future. Through Dad she had ties to the Dearborn County Republican Party. Surely Judge Lowe, the circuit court judge for whom Dad was riding bailiff, was instrumental in leading her to the decision to run for a county office. This is fine with me as long as she buries any idea of being sheriff again. Mom never asked me about running. When

I read the blurb in *The Lawrenceburg Press* announcing her Republican primary run for the office of Dearborn County Recorder, I am not surprised. Mom's action isn't lost on me. I know she struggles to lay the groundwork for our future.

Mom's decision to run for county recorder is not made on a whim. She announces the run two days before Dad's killer was even captured. The notion of recording the county's affairs lay in her heart even before Dad's fateful death. The sheriff's job was thrown in her lap. She never dreamed that this was her calling.

~

A study of how Mayme kept her husband's records in managing the sheriff's duties was certain evidence that she wanted more, was capable of more. Women in office are few in this time. There had been no female office holders in Dearborn County even after voting rights for women passed in 1920. She always said she could do anything she set her mind to do. With the sheriff's job Mayme stuck her foot in the door. She would now shove the door open to realize her chance as county recorder.

The trial for Herman's murderer will soon start in late April or early May, and the campaigning for primary election in May is underway. Problems are arising with the trial. Anderson's attorneys demand a change of venue. The trial moves from Dearborn County to nearby Franklin County at the courthouse in Brookville. Demands of the trial preparations are nipping at Mayme's heels. There is little if any time for her to attend to her future. Knowing the importance of meeting and greeting in the political arena, she places the following ad in

The Lawrenceburg Press prior to the primary election.
To the Voters of Dearborn County

> *My inability to meet every voter in Dearborn County has been my only reason for not doing so. It was my earnest intention to try and see all of you, but the will cannot always be stronger than the body. In my race for the nomination for County Recorder on the Republican ticket, I have avoided personalities, tried to make a clean contest, and now I ask your favorable consideration of my candidacy. If nominated and elected my duty shall be first and always to the people of the County.*
> *Thank you. Mrs. Mayme Lange* [45]

Although she cannot reach every voter personally, Mayme touches them somehow. She handily beats her opponent in the primary for County Recorder by a vote of 1652 to 413. She has more votes for Recorder than any candidate for any other position. With the primary win in hand, Mayme and Stella await the beginning of the Anderson trial.

Even with this great margin of victory, it seems that a November win may not be in the cards. The trial will surely draw a great deal of Mayme's focus and emotion. A woman winning county office, or any office, holds no precedent. With the odds stacked against her, she proceeds. There are no words of "Woe is me", or "How will I ever do it." She puts her back into the plow and her face to the wind. "Bring it on!" The fields won't wait till tomorrow.

~

---

[45] The *Lawrenceburg Press,* 01 May 1930

Mayme Gesell Lange

I just don't know how she does this. Sometimes Mom amazes me.

14

"Preparing for Trial, Case No. 3603"

The upcoming trial for Dad's murderer is the topic of conversation everywhere. I hope to escape the commotion at school. It is futile. The trial is even the subject matter of our social studies class. I just want to hide from it all.

Stella Mae Lange – *My Journal, 03/31/1930*

The choral group has practice all week for the upcoming play. I don't practice singing around the house as there are too many strange people in and out all the time. I'll be coming home late from school, but that's okay. Mom will be glad to not have me under foot. She will be free to talk to all the strangers. I like knowing what is going on, but I don't always understand all the conversations swirling around the jail.

Just yesterday Mom had a couple of visitors, Circuit Court Judge Ricketts and Assistant Prosecuting Attorney Judge Lowe. I know it was them because I see them quite often at the jail, and also because Mom introduced me to them. She says we will see them a great deal before the trial begins. Right now they are concerned that the trial may be moved out of Dearborn County. I don't think that would be a bad thing, and I don't believe Mom would be upset with that outcome. The courthouse sits next door to our home. I dread the notion of seeing Dad's murderer and a lot of other bad characters all the time in our backyard during the trial. They will probably bring Anderson back to our jail during the trial. That thought scares me.

As progress toward the trial continues, Mom takes this afternoon to help me understand what will happen. I trust Mom to tell me what is happening, but I am not always sure I want to know all the details. She pulls out some trial related court documents to help me understand what is being done and what may be done as the trial date moves closer. I know Judge Lowe has prepared Mom for all this as she talks to me in many of his own words.

~

C. W. Napier of Hazard, Kentucky represents James Anderson, the defendant. Napier had been Prosecuting Attorney for the thirty-third Judicial District in Perry County. He is an able lawyer, an earnest and conscientious prosecutor. He is cautious but fearless in the discharge of his sworn duty. His abilities will certainly test the team prosecuting Herman's case.[46]

First thing, Napier attempts to have the three possible Dearborn County judges removed from the trial. Court records of The State of Indiana vs. James Anderson, No. 3603, show the following action by Napier.

"And now again come the State of Indiana, by Julius Schwing, Prosecuting Attorney and Charles A. Lowe, its attorneys, and said defendant in his own proper person and by

---

[46] Louis Pilcher, *The Story of Hazard, Kentucky, The Pearl of the Mountain,* June 1913

C. W. Napier, his attorney, comes also, and said defendant having filed his motion and affidavit for a change of venue from the Judge of this court and the court having examined the same, finds said motion and affidavit in due form and sufficient and now grants the prayer thereof and does now grant to said defendant a change of Judge as prayed for in said petition and does now nominate Martin J. Givan, Hon. Estal G Bielby, and Hon. Cassius W. McMullen, three competent and disinterested persons, each of whom is an available member of the bar of the State of Indiana, and does now submit said list of names of said persons so nominated to be submitted to the parties to the action and thereupon the State of Indiana by its attorneys strike from said list the name of Hon. Martin J. Givan, and thereupon said defendant by his attorney now asks that he be given until 1 o'clock P. M. of this day before striking off one of the said names, which said request is now by court granted.

And afterwards at said 1 o'clock P.M. comes said defendant by his attorney and orally objects to the name of Hon. Estal G. Bielby, remaining on said list and asking that the court substitute another name instead of the name of Estal G. Bielby, and this matter is now submitted to and taken by the court under advisement until 9 o'clock A.M. tomorrow. " [47]

The reasons for withdrawal of certain judges are twofold. First, the judges reside in the county in which Herman Lange served. They may be influenced by friends and neighbors and relatives of the deceased in favor of the State of Indiana in any rulings they would make. The second reason deals especially with Estal G. Bielby. He has refused to accept legal employment for Walter Anderson, brother of James Anderson.

---

[47] *State of Indiana vs. James Anderson, No. 3603,* Dearborn County Circuit Court, 26 March 1930

This judge has also expressed his opinion derogatory to the interest of the defendant, James Anderson.

~

I don't understand how people close to Dad can be expected to be impartial. They loved him.

~

Things proceed quickly. Judge William Ricketts is disqualified from serving as Judge in the case of The State of Indiana vs. James Anderson. Estal Bielby is removed from the case. Hon. Cassius McMullen is removed from the case. March 31, 1930, proffers Martin J. Givan appointed special Judge of the court in case 3603. Givan is sworn in as Judge of the Dearborn County Circuit Court in the Anderson Case.

Judge Lowe and Prosecutor Julius Schwing line up their witnesses. George Adam Knosp, "Spike", serving time at the Indiana Penal Farm is put under bond and ordered to appear as a witness for the state when the trial begins. Walter Anderson, the defendant's brother, is also ordered to be held in the Dearborn County Jail as a material witness for the State during the trial.

Judges removed, criminal witnesses held, new judge appointed. Pretrial work marches to completion. One last flurry of activity by the defense begs to have the trial taken away from Dearborn County. Martin J. Given, Special Judge, on April 21, 1930, assigns the venue of the case to be moved away from Dearborn County.

"And now comes the defendant and presents and files his

motion and affidavit for a change of venue of this cause from Dearborn County, which said motion and affidavit respectfully reads as follows and the court having seen and examined the said motion and affidavit grants the prayer thereof, and now orders the venue of this cause changed from Dearborn county, Indiana; and the court now finds and determines that Franklin County is the most convenient county for the trial of this cause, and now orders that the venue of this cause be and the same is now changed to Franklin County in the State of Indiana.

It is further ordered by the court that the clerk of this court immediately make up a complete transcript of the proceedings and orders of the court in this cause, and properly certify the same; that seal the said transcript up with the original papers in this cause, and deliver the same to the Sheriff of Dearborn County, Indiana; that upon the receipt of the said transcript and original papers the Sheriff of Dearborn County, without delay, shall deliver the said transcript and original papers to the Clerk of the Circuit Court of Franklin County, Indiana, at Brookville and make return to the Clerk of this Court showing such delivery and deposit.

It is further ordered and adjudged by the court that the Sheriff of Dearborn County, Indiana, transfer and deliver the custody of the defendant, James Anderson, to the Sheriff of Franklin County, Indiana, together with a certified copy of this order; and the Clerk of this court is now ordered and directed to make up and issue the necessary and proper writs and copies for the carrying of this order unto effect." [48]

Little concern appears to be entertained for the fact that Mayme, now sheriff of Dearborn County, was born and raised

---

[48] *State of Indiana vs. James Anderson, No. 3603,* Dearborn County Circuit Court, 21 April 19

in Franklin County. Her parents lived just a few short miles from the Franklin County seat of Brookville. Gesell and Franzman relatives are spread all across the county. These relatives and their friends and their neighbors will shower support upon Mayme and Stella. Impartiality may be a difficult thing to find anywhere in the counties surrounding Dearborn.

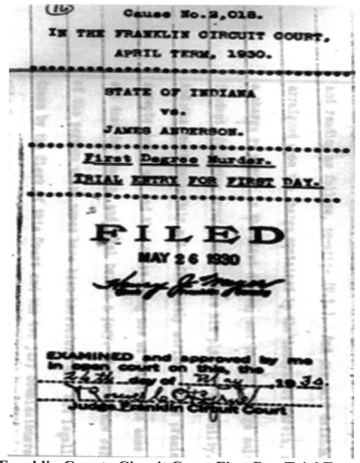

Franklin County Circuit Court First Day Trial Entry

With the venue changed, April 22, 1930 becomes moving day. Mayme will bring Dearborn County court documents to the new trial site in Franklin County as duty demands in the murder of Herman. The move to Franklin County brings another attorney to the defendant. William L. Chambers, an attorney from Brookville, joins in the defense with C. W. Napier. On April 23 the court orders the defendant held in custody by the Sheriff of Decatur County. The last piece of the pretrial fits into place. The Sheriff is ordered to deliver the defendant, James Anderson, to the Franklin County Jail no later than 6:00 P.M. on May 25. Sheriff Personette of Franklin County and Deputy Sheriff James Hulbert of Dearborn County will deliver James Anderson to the Franklin County Jail on Sunday, May 25. Case 2018 is on the Docket of the Franklin Circuit Court to begin at 9:00 A.M. on Monday May 26, 1930.

Judge Roscoe C. O'Byrne

The judge hearing the case for the Circuit Court of Franklin County is Roscoe C. O'Byrne, appointed to the court in 1928. He graduated from the Indiana School of Law. All eyes in Franklin and Dearborn Counties will follow the judge's every action. In his two years in the court the judge has heard no murder trial. Case number 2018 will be Roscoe C. O'Byrne's first time presiding over a first degree murder trial. This will be his most important trial in his term as circuit court judge. The people expect a fair trial, a swift trial, but more than anything a verdict of guilty to atone for the attack on their sheriff. Judge Roscoe C. O'Byrne is about to get the greatest test of his term as judge of the circuit court of Franklin County.

~

Mom tries to help me understand what is happening. I am not so sure. What I really understand is my need to practice for the play. It's next week and I want to do great. I hope Mom invites Aunt Betty to the show. Betty is a great singer herself, and sure to enjoy our performance.

15

"State of Indiana vs. James Anderson"
<u>Day One Case Number 2018</u>

Mom says I don't have to go to school. I can travel with her to Brookville to watch the trial of Dad's murderer. The thought of being in the same room with the killer looking at me scares me. Everyone says it will be over quickly. I'll go, but only to see Mom's relatives.

Stella Mae Lange – My Journal, 05/25/1930

Mom's driving us to Brookville after church Sunday. We're going to stay with Aunt Susie. I haven't seen my Cousin Millie since last summer. I know we will probably be at the courthouse every day, but I certainly hope I can go horse-back riding with Millie. I haven't been on a horse since we left the farm to live at the jail. I sure do miss that. I miss Blackie too.

I enjoy the evening's dinner with Susie, George, and Millie. I think Mom ordered everyone not to speak about the trial tomorrow. We all retire to the living room after dinner for an entertaining evening listening to the *Buster Brown Show* on Uncle George's new Philco radio. Buster Brown and his dog Tige entertain us with grand fun. When "Froggie plunks his magic twanger" Millie and I fall off our chairs. I guess we go a little overboard as we are each sent to bed shortly after that. Millie and I will sit up in her bed talking till daylight if they let us.

Outdoors a summer is greening. I rise and head downstairs for breakfast, discovering Mom has already left for the courthouse. I guess she doesn't want to miss anything. I am in no hurry. I can wait. I'll go over with Aunt Susie right before things get started at 9:00 a.m.

Susie and I arrive at the courthouse where we meet Deputy Lafe Perpimgton, who escorts us in through a backdoor to avoid the crowds out on the street. I have never seen that many people at our Dearborn County Courthouse. I suppose I never realized the importance of this trial. It must mean a lot to more people than just Mom and me. My heart beats a little faster as Susie leads me in the back door and up the steps. I can barely catch my breath as we climb each and every marble step. There are people all over this place.

Lafe pushes into the courtroom and ushers us up through a maze of grim faces to a bench at the front of the room where Mom stands talking to Judge Lowe. The judge grabs my hand and smiles at me as Susie sits me down at the end of the bench. I sit and look around. There are so many strange faces to absorb I cannot focus on any one. The blur of activity in the room is a little dizzying. I close my eyes and try to ease my queasy head. Mom sits down beside me and puts her arm around my shoulder.

Two armed deputies enter the room astride the scruffy looking young man I had seen at the jail many weeks before. As he walks with his guards, he turns his head toward me. I see those cold dark eyes again staring straight through me. I shiver as the fear overtakes me. No sooner do the three men pass me, when I see everyone turn to the front of the room.

The Judge enters. A voice in the front of the room booms out that we must all rise for the Honorable Judge Roscoe C. O'Byrne. The judge beats his gavel on his wood desk and the booming voice orders us to be seated. I close my eyes tighter and sit down. I try to shut it all out.

~

Franklin County Court Room Brookville, Indiana

It is Monday morning 9:00 A.M. in the court room of Franklin County Circuit Court Judge Roscoe C. O'Byrne. All the cast members of the drama of *State of Indiana vs. James Anderson*, Case number 2018 are assembled. Attorneys for the plaintiff, Charles A. Lowe, Julius G. Schwing, and Charles R. Baker are there. Attorneys for the defendant C. W. Napier and William L. Chambers are there. Sheriff Mayme Lange and her daughter Stella Mae are there. Deputy Sheriff James Hulbert of

Dearborn County and Sheriff Personette of Franklin County are there. Chief Investigating Detective Ora Slater and many other law enforcement and judicial officials of Dearborn County are present. The small county courtroom is crowded—filled to capacity with over 100 people outside unable to gain admission. Interest in the outcome, anxious for justice, and respect for Herman, Mayme, and Stella fill the court room.

The courtroom buzzes with activity. Every seat is filled. Every person whispers. Hems and haws and coughs and muted conversations fill the room. Every eye focuses on the accused sitting with his attorneys at the table in the front of the room. Judge O'Byrne shuffles papers on his desk and court is in session. The room goes quiet. Case number 2018 begins.

The trial begins with the defendant being arraigned. Defense Attorney C. W. Napier pleads not guilty for James Anderson. This appears to be a far different tune than the one sung by Anderson in his March 15 confession. The defense claims that Anderson's signed confession was taken under duress. They also file a motion for a new trial. The defense plea of innocence sets the court room abuzz. The judge pounds the desk with his gavel. He orders the room to be quiet once more. With this plea of not guilty, the State must now take its desired outcome of murder in the first degree before a jury. Immediately following this posturing by the defense, jury selection begins. The question of twelve people free of preconceived opinions about the greatest murder in Dearborn County history was answered with the change of the trial from Dearborn County to neighboring Franklin. Now the art of picking a jury begins. Each side has an idea of what they want in the perfect juror.

Sixty-five possible jurors are called for the first day of

the trial. The attorneys question and the press scrutinize each juror. Every name on the list of prospective jurors is that of a man. There are no women in the jury pool. This must be a mistake. This action is not lost with Mayme. She understands the potential empathy for a widow's loss. Who would profit from women on the jury, plaintiff or defense? The right of a woman to serve on a jury was established in Indiana in 1920 at the same time she was accorded the right to vote. [49]

In a long back and forth struggle between plaintiff and defense, juror interviews consume the entire day. The plaintiff for the state requires belief in the death penalty to be imperative for a juror to be acceptable. The defense needs jurors with few or no ties to nearby Dearborn County. An indifference to Prohibition also serves well in the plans of the defense. Each side displays a serious interest in the reading habits of every potential juror. What do they know of the elements of the case?   Charles Lowe questions whether any potential juror opposes capital punishment. He asks time after time, "Would you flinch from a verdict which would send this young man to the electric chair?" Any hesitance in answering this query brings immediate dismissal from the jury pool by the prosecution.

Defense Attorney Napier asks, "Mr. Rauch, do you own a gun?"

Potential Juror Henry Rauch answers, "Yes. I hunt in the fall."

Prosecuting Attorney Lowe asks, "Mr. Brackney, must you hear Mr. Anderson's testimony in order to determine guilt?"

---

[49] Burnita Shelton Matthews, "The Woman Juror", *Women Lawyers' Journal Vol. 15, No.2,* January 1927

Potential Juror George Brackney answers, "Not if there is sufficient evidence to help me make a decision."

So goes the back and forth of questioning for each juror throughout the first day. Conflicts of interest, dismissals for cause, and peremptory challenges eliminate thirty-nine potential jurors from possible participation in this trial. Defense lawyers seem to fear that members of the pool may be too close to the victim's family.

As the first day of trial draws to a close, forty-six members of the jury pool had been interviewed. Only seven jurors were agreed upon and selected. Judge O'Byrne orders examination of jurors to continue on the next day.

~

Mom shakes me. I'm not really sleeping. My eyes are open but I see none of the day's activities. I walk out between Mom and Susie. We head back to George and Susi's home for dinner. Mom helps Susi with some soup and vegetables they had prepared the night before. We all sit quietly and eat our meal. A neighbor had brought a pie over earlier and we pretend to enjoy it. A long day in the tense atmosphere of the courtroom leaves all of us drained. After supper, I go with Millie to her room. We start a conversation about school but we never finish. I am asleep on the bed in my clothes.

16

"State of Indiana vs. James Anderson"
Day Two Case Number 2018

Yesterday's jury selection put me to sleep. It was so boring. That's a good thing for me. I don't want to be here.
Stella Mae Lange – *My Journal, 05/27/1930*

I have no patience for another day of jury selection. The same questions over and over. The same faces over and over. I catch Anderson's dark eyes across the room. I shut down.

~

On Tuesday, May 27, trial resumes again. Once more jury selection is the order of business. Still no potential women jurors. The slow, deliberative process drags on.

C. W. Napier showed himself to be a good listener on the first day of jury selection. He asked pointed questions but allowed jurors time to answer. He never once put words into anyone's mouth. He knew he was dealing with a group that probably knew Herman and his wife very well, thus he was careful choosing his words. He offended no one with his probing words.

Charles Lowe worked on his best homespun humor. He played to the jury like Douglas Fairbanks to Mary Pickford, tugging at their heartstrings. He wore his personal investment in the search for justice for the sheriff's family on his sleeve like a badge of honor and dedication. His questions to prospective jurors left no doubt of his love for the deceased.

Defense Attorney Napier asks, "Mr. Wolber, do you own a gun?"

Potential Juror William Wolber answers, "Yes, I do."

"Do you hunt?"

"Nope."

"If you were in physical danger could you fire your to gun to protect yourself or your family?"

"Yep, I would."

"Thank you, Mr. Wolber."

Prosecuting Attorney Lowe asks, "Mr. Wolber, if the defendant is found guilty can you agree with a sentence of the death penalty?"

William Wolber answers, "Yes, I can. I believe that the Bible calls for an eye for an eye."

Back and forth go the attorneys—question after question, juror after juror. At the end of the day, 39 more jury candidates are interviewed with four being chosen. In less than two days 77 people fill eleven seats. It will take a third day to finish interviews and fill all jury seats.

~

I never thought finding twelve people to fill a jury in Franklin County would be so difficult. This better not be an indication of what will happen in the rest of the trial.

17

"State of Indiana vs. James Anderson"
Day Three Case Number 2018

*Seating a jury in Franklin County should be easy. This is not
what I expected.*

Stella Mae Lange – *My Journal, 05/28/1930*

My mind sleeps through another day. I'm in the courtroom
in body only. What I don't see and what I don't hear
won't hurt me. Susi nudges me at lunch time, but that is all I
wake for.

~

Wednesday, May 28, jury selection continues. More than one
hundred people have been quizzed since the beginning of the
trial. Questioning of prospective jurors drags on till lunch.
After the break, the intense grilling of jurors begins again.

Defense Attorney Napier asks, "Mr. Cloud, do you
know any of the victim's family? Do you know any of the
Langes or Gesells?"

Potential Juror Bert Cloud answers, "No, I don't. I know
of some of the Gesell's at the church in Klemmes Corner, but

none of them are immediate family."

Prosecuting Attorney Lowe asks, "Mr. Cloud, how long have you lived in Posey Township?"

Bert Cloud answers, "All my life."

"Have you ever been arrested?"

"Never."

Prosecuting Attorney Lowe finishes with the juror. He has no challenges to Mr. Cloud being added to the jury.

Finally, a jury of twelve men and no women was selected and impaneled. To be sworn in and rule on Case no. 2018, State of Indiana vs. James Anderson, are the following twelve men: Henry Rauch, George Brackney, Frank Forrester, Christ Sottong, Charles Shafer, Alexander Crawford, Joseph Ortman, William H. Wolber, John Calpha, Frank Meyer, Lewis Schreiner, and Bert Cloud. It is amazing that none of the jurors is related in any way to Mayme Lange. With the jury seated, trial activity begins.

Without withdrawal or request for withdrawal of the plea, the defendant's attorneys', Napier and Chambers, file and present written action to quash, to overthrow the indictment.

It is unclear where Napier and Chambers are heading. Perhaps they believe their defendant, James Anderson, shot Herman Lange in self-defense. Judge O'Byrne denies the motion. Witnesses are sworn and the court orders separation of witnesses.

The State makes its opening statement to the jury. Charles Lowe and Julius Schwing, attorneys for the plaintiff, make an impassioned plea for the conviction of the accused murderer of their beloved sheriff and dear friend to be adjudicated and justice served. They offer that their greatest and most damning evidence will be Herman Lange's "Dying

Statement" and James Anderson's signed confession. Dearborn's judicial and law enforcement officials, neighbors, friends and colleagues of Herman are in the courtroom. Both Lawrenceburg newspapers report the Courthouse is filled to overflowing again. The pain of Herman's loss is great. The reading of the dying man's last statement wrings tears from the hearts of the people of Dearborn County.

The Court gives counsel for James Anderson the opportunity to give the defendant's opening statement to the jury. Napier and Chambers decline to present the defendant's opening statement. Judge O'Byrne warns the defense that no such opening statement at any later date during the trial will be permitted by the Court. It's now or never. With the defense making no opening statement, they also object to the action of the Court in restricting them from making that statement later. With the State ready to introduce its evidence time wanes and proceedings are set to begin again on the next day. This passionate case is off to a bumpy start.

~

I can't believe all the questions they asked the jurors. I can't believe they had to question so many to find people they could trust to do the job of judging the guilt of Dad's murderer.

18

"State of Indiana vs. James Anderson"
<u>Day Four Case Number 2018</u>

We have a jury. Mom said that things will proceed quickly from here.

Stella Mae Lange – *My Journal, 05/29/1930*

I don't think I can put up with this anymore. They are going to begin bringing in witnesses today. I can't bear the thought of listening to the man who shot Dad. I know Mom wants me to be here, but it is painful for me. I will close my eyes still again. Perhaps I can find a better place to be.

~

38Caliber Smith and Wesson WWI Army Revolver

The court's bailiff brings an exhibit to the front of the room and places it on the table in front of the judge's bench. The exhibit is an old Smith and Wesson 38 caliber Army revolver. The prosecution will establish this exhibit as the same gun used to kill Dearborn County Sheriff Herman Lange.

On the first day of evidence for the State, the attorneys for the plaintiff call George Knosp to the stand. George is better known as "Spike", at whose camp the trio of James Anderson, Gus Seiter, and Roscoe Bradburn had disagreements and were asked to leave. George was brought to the courtroom from the Indiana Penal Farm in Putnamville. He was sent to the farm after his camp was raided and shut down in early January. Knosp is a hostile witness, but his testimony is vital in placing Anderson at the camp.

Prosecuting Attorney Lowe asks George Knosp, "Do people know you as 'Spike'?"

Witness George Knosp answers, "Yep, that's what they call me."

"Did you run a camp on the Whitewater River near Harrison?"

"'Til they went and put a padlock on it in January."

"Did you sell liquor there?"

"You all know that's illegal. There may have been some people brought their own in. I'd never sell it to 'em."

"Okay, so there were people drinking at your camp?"

"Yep."

"Was this man over here (the Prosecuting Attorney points to the defendant, James Anderson) in your place on the evening of December 29?"

"Yep, that'd be him."

"Was he drinking that evening?"

"Yep, he and a couple of his friends had their own flasks. They seemed to be in pretty good spirits when they walked in the door."

"Did James Anderson get in a fight?"

"He got pretty rowdy. I saw he had a gun and I took it away from him."

"Is this the gun (Prosecuting Attorney points to the gun on the table before the judge) you saw Mr. Anderson with?"

"Yep, that looks like it."

"Did he have that gun when he left?"

"Yep. He got in another argument with someone and I threw him and his buddies out. I gave Anderson back his gun when they left."

George's testimony confirms that James Anderson had the gun when he left the establishment on the river. This places the gun in Anderson's hand when shots were fired through the door at "Spike's" camp.

Prosecuting Attorney Lowe speaks to the jury, "Let it be known that the bullet removed from the leg of Benjamin Shaw, the man injured by a shot through the door as Anderson left the camp, is the same caliber as that of the gun that the defendant had when he left."

Lafe Perpington, Herman's deputy, also testifies on this first evidentiary day. He describes the condition of Benjamin Shaw—shot through the door at "Spike's" camp. The wound was serious, a bullet lodged in the victim's groin. Lafe had interviewed Seiter and Bradburn, Anderson's companions, and describes how he and Herman brought them back to the Dearborn Jail. He described Seiter and Bradburn as nervous, talkative and eager to declare their companion Anderson as Shaw's assailant. Lafe describes the sheriff's anxious return to search for the shooter.

Prosecuting Attorney Lowe asks Lafe, "Were you with the sheriff when he brought the prisoners, Seiter and Bradburn, to the Lawrenceburg Jail?"

Deputy Perpington answers, "Yes, I was. I locked 'em in the cell while Herman gave Mayme information for the Arrest Log."

"Then what?"

"I told the sheriff we should wait until morning light to go after Anderson. Herman wanted to leave right away. He told me to stay with the prisoners and he'd go out to try to pick up the shooter's scent."

"And what did the sheriff do next?"

"He took off back toward the Whitewater camps to find Anderson."

The Judge adjourned for the day. Trial would start anew in the morning.

~

I open my eyes long enough to see that gun that was used to shoot Dad. They don't talk about it, but I know they will tomorrow. I know I can't do this. I'm going to ask Mom tonight if I can skip court tomorrow.

19

"State of Indiana vs. James Anderson"
Day Five Case Number 2018

It's Decoration Day today and we're stuck in the courthouse.
What a terrible way to celebrate this beginning of summer.
Stella Mae Lange – *My Journal, 05/30/1930*

I'm back. Mom says I must stay. She doesn't want me to be alone and worry—so I will sit in the courtroom and worry.

~

On day two of evidence Gus Seiter and Roscoe Bradburn are questioned as to their part in the disturbance at "Spike's". They place Anderson with the gun and point to him as the shooter of Benjamin Shaw.

Prosecuting Attorney Lowe asks Seiter, "Why were you and your friends asked to leave 'Spikes' on the early morning of December 30?"

Witness Gus Seiter responded, "James was drunk and wanted only to fight. George had taken away his gun earlier, but James was still fighting."

"So what happened when you were asked to leave?"

"Jim really flew off the handle. He yelled that George was not going to throw him out."

"Did George throw you out?"

"Yes. He told James to get lost and to take us with him. George gave the gun back and showed us the door."

"Did you all leave then?"

"Well, we headed to the door, but when we got outside and the door slammed shut, James blew his top. He fired off a couple of quick shots into the door."

"What then?"

"Somebody inside yelled that a man had been wounded. We didn't see no one get shot, but James got real panicked and took off running. Just then someone grabbed me and Roscoe so we couldn't run."

Lowe asked Bradburn the same questions. Roscoe corroborated his friend's story. The morning's testimony puts Anderson with the gun, the anger, the shooting, and now on the run into the night.

The afternoon of day two evidence, the State questions Tom Maines and his wife Emma. These two brought Herman into their farm house after he had been shot nearby. Herman's statement to them that he was badly injured and knew he was mortally wounded corroborates Herman's frame of mind in his later "dying declaration". Emma testifies that she heard some shooting near her home. She heard Lange holler "Oh Help me" and "Oh, my God help me"; but that she did not know who it was calling for help.

Herman came to the door of their home and told Tom Maines who he was. He cried "My God help me, I am shot."

They brought Herman into the house and noticed that his

fingers were shot. Emma assisted Herman into a bed and asked what hurt?" She told of Herman's answer, "It is killing me. I won't get over this."

The Maine's' also testify that they saw considerable blood on the sheriff's coat. Their statements are vital to the State showing the severity of Herman's condition.

~

I woke up long enough to see Bradburn and Seiter on the stand. I didn't like seeing them housed in our jail. I didn't like seeing them here today.

I walk out from the Courthouse into the street where summer blooms. What I'd give just to have one day for a picnic with friends under one of the big old Maple trees on the farm.

20

"State of Indiana vs. James Anderson"
Day Six Case Number 2018

Not much of a Memorial Day celebration. We didn't even see any fireworks last night.

Stella Mae Lange – *My Journal, 05/31/1930*

Mom does not let me stay away. She says it is important that I see justice done for Dad. I understand her sense of duty, but I don't think she understands my fearful feelings. I get chills each time I see that man who killed Dad. I go to the courtroom. I shut my eyes yet again.

~

Saturday May 31, brings day three of testimony. Court proceedings on Saturday? Is this a rush to judgment? Today begins with Dr. Sheets of Harrison describing the severity of Herman's condition. The doctor came to the Maines' house to treat Herman; and when he saw how badly he was wounded, he had him transported to Cincinnati Bethesda Hospital.

Dr. Shewman, a surgeon of Cincinnati, testifies that Herman was brought to Bethesda Hospital on December 30,

147

about 8:40 a. m. He states that the sheriff was suffering from a 38 caliber bullet wound in the abdomen. While Herman was conscious when brought in and continued so up until the time of his death, there were periods when he drifted in and out of consciousness. The bullet had entered the abdomen about two and one-half inches above the umbilicus. It passed through the abdominal wall and through the peritoneum and buried itself in the muscles of the back.

Prosecuting Attorney Lowe asks Doctor Shewman, "Were you on duty at Bethesda Hospital on the morning of December 30?"

Witness Doctor Shewman responds, "I was lead emergency room surgeon that morning."

"Do you remember treating Sheriff Herman Lange on that morning?"

"I did treat Mr. Lange. He had lost a great deal of blood. The bullet had done a lot of damage to his intestines. I did surgery to try to assess the damage and fix what I could. There was no way to undo the great damage that had been done."

"Did you believe he would survive his wounds?"

"There was no way he would live. He had only a short time to live. I told him of his situation and suggested he prepare for the worst."

The final Saturday witness is Dearborn County coroner Doctor, C. C. Marshall who describes the wounds that caused the sheriff's death. The Doctor hinted that Herman would have died at the Maines' farm if he had not had treatment. He said that the sheriff would die. It was just a case of how soon.

The judge ended today's proceedings after both doctors' somber testimony. The court room emptied silently this afternoon.

~

Tomorrow is Sunday. Thank goodness there will be no court proceedings on the Lord's Day. I would rather spend the entire day at church than sit in court.

21

"Day of Rest"

No trial on Sunday. Peace at last.
                    Stella Mae Lange – *My Journal, 06/01/1930*

It was so nice not sitting in that dreary courtroom on Sunday. We all go to Church this morning. Mom's head bows throughout the service—is it prayer or is it worry? Mom doesn't linger long after services. She isn't of a mood to answer all the questions of the happening in the trial. I can't blame her.

It's back to the farm for breakfast. Millie and I plan our afternoon adventures. We will get the horse out and ride around the farm. What a great way to shake the cobwebs clouding my mind from the drudgery of the trial—a bright sun and a fast horse. Millie and I enjoy the peace. Susi makes a nice chicken dinner to top off the day. Tonight I dread tomorrow.

22

"State of Indiana vs. James Anderson"
<u>Day Seven Case Number 2018</u>

We had a relaxing afternoon at the farm. I needed that.
Stella Mae Lange – *My Journal, 06/01/1930*

The day away from the courtroom has not improved my mood. Yesterday only made me more anxious to be anywhere but here. This is no way to spend my summer vacation.

~

On day four Walter Anderson and Leonard Burch are called to take the stand. Anderson is the defendant's brother and Burch is his brother-in-law. Each helped James Anderson escape and misled law enforcement on their search for the suspect.

Prosecuting Attorney Lowe asks witness Walter Anderson, "On the morning of December 30 did you help your brother James Anderson hide from the authorities?"

Witness Anderson responded, "I don't remember."

"Let me ask you again. Did you help your brother escape?"

"I don't remember."

Lowe asks Leonard Burch the same questions and gets no response. They don't want to answer the questions. The Judge threatens more jail time if they don't start to participate. Frustrated, the Judge orders the witnesses from the courtroom. He recesses the court for lunch.

Upon return, the Judge again orders the witnesses to cooperate or return to jail. They give in and give up and testify.

~

What a bad, bad day. I can see the summer sun out the courtroom window. I can't enjoy it.

23

"State of Indiana vs. James Anderson"
Day Eight Case Number 2018

I remember feeding those guys, Burch and Anderson, when they were held at our jail. I didn't like them then and I don't like them now.

Stella Mae Lange – *My Journal, 06/02/1930*

U p early again. I really want to sleep in. School is out for summer and I'm stuck here at the courthouse. How much longer do I need to suffer through this? Surely, enough has been shown to convict Dad's killer.

~

For more than five days, from May 29 through June 2, attorneys Schwing, Lowe, and Baker bring evidence to prove the State's case. their evidence is all circumstantial with one exception—the eye witness account of one person, that is the "dying declaration" of Sheriff Herman T. Lange. Five days of evidence and testimony brought by attorneys for the plaintiff. The State's success in their case rests on the shoulders of Herman's "dying declaration."

Day five's evidence appears to be important. Ora Slater, Chief Investigating Detective in the case, takes the stand. He took Herman's "dying declaration" at Bethesda Hospital. Slater reads the dying sheriff's statement to the court. Eyes fill with tears as he speaks. He states that he and others were at the hospital about 4:00 p.m. on December 31. He saw Herman. The Sheriff realized that he was close to death. Julius Schwing, Judge Lowe, and Howard Shearer were also present. They talked to Herman, and then made a typewritten statement of what had happened on the road near Longenecker Station. Slater, Schwing, Lowe, and Shearer testify that the written statement was read to Herman. He said it was a true statement, and he signed.

Prior to continuing with evidence, Judge O'Byrne asks the bailiff to escort the jury out of the court room. The defense wishes Anderson's signed confession to be dismissed as evidence since the defendant changed his story. The Judge hears testimony from all the main players in the gathering of the signed confession. Ora slater, James Hulbert, Sheriff Coy of Greensburg, and court reporter Edward Kurtzman are the state's principal witnesses to the validity of Anderson's confession. The Judge believes that this confession was made with no promises, threats, or coercion and can be used as evidence before the jury. When the state's witnesses are cross examined as to the signed confession, some of them seem to be a little confused about the events at the Versailles and the Greensburg jails.

Slater is one of the primary witnesses in James Anderson's voluntary confession at the Greensburg Jail in Decatur County. Slater knows it all and has all the facts. He is a compelling witness. He pulls out all his persuasive interrogative techniques and uses them to win the hearts of the jurors.

Ora was also instrumental in the search for and arrest of James Anderson. Slater leads the jury through the backwoods and hills of Kentucky in describing his search for Anderson. You can almost feel the prickly cockleburs biting at your ankles and the jagged pebble stuck in your shoe grinding at your heel as Ora painted the picture of the craggy paths and rugged hills the searchers trudged over to ferret out the running Anderson.

He unloads his frustration with law enforcement of Rock Castle County, Kentucky playing a game of 'hide n seek' with the posse in search of Herman's killer. Slater allowed his searing emotions to boil over to the jury, descrying, "A man innocent of murder does not run up and down the god-forsaken terrain of southern Kentucky hiding from the truth. James Anderson is guilty as sin and we caught him."

The judge gaveled an end to the day and the courtroom emptied without a whisper.

~

I open my eyes long enough today to listen to Detective Slater. He certainly is a smooth talker. Mom says he'd be rich if he had become a salesman instead of a detective. I know he convinced everyone of Anderson's guilt. Hopefully all will be over soon.

24

"State of Indiana vs. James Anderson"
Day Nine Case Number 2018

Someone told me James Anderson would take the stand today.
The thought of listening to him chills my spine.
Stella Mae Lange – My Journal, 06/03/1930

Mr. Slater stopped me as I entered the courtroom with Susie.He took my hand, promising he would do his part to bring justice. For just a second I stood straight and steady.

~

On day six of testimony, the defense begins their presentation. Napier and Chambers call their defendant to the stand. Perhaps they call upon Anderson to dispute Herman's "dying declaration"—stating that his coat blew open and his sheriff's badge was readily visible to the man standing before him. Maybe they just want Anderson to muddy the waters enough to confuse the jurors. *The Brookville Democrat* in its June 5, 1930 edition brings the following account of James Anderson as he takes the witness stand.

Anderson took the stand as the final witness for the

defense, Wednesday, declaring he had been induced to make the confession because of fear of mob violence. He claimed he had told the truth at the Versailles jail and the officials had refused to accept it. He declared that on the trip from Versailles to the Greensburg jail, he was told of the electric chair which was used in this state and that he would be given three days in which to talk. He further claimed it was because of these threats and intimations that he had signed the confession which was not true in its entirety.

According to defendant's story, the sheriff had proffered him a lift and when he started to get in the car, the sheriff came around the rear of the machine with a flashlight in one hand and a pistol in the other and that he (Anderson) had shot in self-defense, not knowing that it was an officer of the law.[50]

Judge Lowe stopped Anderson's testimony a number of times. The prosecuting attorney is in red-faced denial of Anderson's recanting of his confession. Charles Lowe pounds his fist into the table and objects time and again as Anderson speaks. His passion to serve justice for his friend Herman burns in his voice. He is relentless in his challenges to the defense. Lowe continues to shout till Judge O'Byrne gavels the end of the day's proceedings. Spent, Charles collapses in his chair.

~

I can't believe they allowed Anderson to lie about his encounter with Dad. He shot Dad, no questions asked. Mom's face is a knot of anger and disapproval, but her grey eyes appear to be coming from somewhere else, two pools of expectation. I can't handle this.

---

[50] *The Brookville Democrat,* 05 June 1930 1

25

"State of Indiana vs. James Anderson"
Day Ten Case Number 2018

Yesterday was so disturbing listening to that man call my Father a liar.

Stella Mae Lange – *My Journal June 04, 1930*

I can't put up with this. Please be done. This is all a bad dream. Something happens every day—nothing good.

~

On day seven of testimony C. W. Napier completes his interview of the defendant. Charles Lowe will now get his chance to confront his friend's murderer. He reminds himself silently to be professional and calm. He believes he has a conviction in hand. It is hard to keep his feelings buried. He brought Herman to this job. He does not want to let him down now. He steals a glance toward Mayme's chair in the courtroom. He steadies his voice and begins.

Prosecuting Attorney Lowe addresses the defendant, "Is your name James Anderson?"

Defendant Anderson responds, "It is."

"Were you at the Whitewater camp named 'Spikes' on the morning of December 30?"

"Yeh."

"Were you with James Seiter and Roscoe Bradburn, two gentlemen seated over there, on that same morning at 'Spikes'?"

"Yeh."

"Did George Knosp take your gun after a fight on that morning?"

"Yeh."

"When you continued to fight, did George return your gun and throw you out of his camp?"

"Yeh."

"Did you shoot through the closed door in anger as you were leaving?"

"Yeh, but I didn't think anyone was'd behind the door?"

Lowe finally gets to the part when Herman met up with Anderson on the Brookville Road in Braysville near Longenecker Station. He steps closer to Anderson. He moves so close to the witness stand that their knees almost touch. Lowe's steely grey eyes stare directly into Anderson's reddened pupils. He blinks once and says, "When you saw Sheriff Lange's coat blow open revealing his badge, you shot him. Didn't you?"

"Nope. It didn't happen that way."

"You shot him just like that. Didn't you?"

"No, no. It was self-defense. I didn't see his badge."

"You shot him. Just like I said."

"No, no, no."

Judge O'Byrne urges Lowe to get back on point and wrap up questioning. The State is satisfied they have all they need to convict. The defense cry of self-defense is a moot point. Lowe has no more emotion to spend. He bows to the Judge's orders and ends his questioning.

~

I cannot sleep. I can only cry. I am tired of this.

26

State of Indiana vs. James Anderson
<u>**Day Eleven Case Number 2018**</u>

Mom says the end is near. I wish I could be so confident.
Stella Mae Lange – *My Journal, June 05, 1930*

One more day, I will be glad when this is done. It will be done, right?

~

With just a little over one day of evidence for the defense presented, hearing of all evidence is complete. June 6, the eleventh day of the trial, both the State and the defendant present to the Court written request for the jury to be instructed. The State and Defense each prepare their closing arguments, carrying final arguments over into the next morning.

~

My head aches. My eyes burn. My back is stiff. I just feel awful.

27

"State of Indiana vs. James Anderson"
Day Twelve Case Number 2018

Can this be it? I have so waited for this day. Will it bring us peace?

Stella Mae Lange – *My Journal, June 06, 1930*

Mom told me last night there would be a verdict today. I can't wait. Today is the day. It will be done.

~

On day twelve, Saturday, June 7, the court room is packed. Mayme and Stella sit in the front row. Law enforcement and judiciary and citizens from Dearborn and its adjoining counties fill the room. So many people attend that a great number must stand outside the court to await the outcome.

Defense Attorney C. W. Napier of Hazard, Kentucky begins with his closing argument. In his statements before the jury, he gives a strong and forceful plea to the jury. He argues the shooting was in self-defense, the story James Anderson told on the witness stand.

Judge Charles Lowe, for whom Herman began his career

as bailiff, presents the closing argument for the State. Herman Lange was a loving husband to Mayme. He was a devoted father to Stella. He was admired by the people of Dearborn County. He was faithful to his sworn duty to uphold the law and defend the people of his county. It was that "faithful enforcement of his sworn duty" that brought him to investigate a shooting at 'Spike's' Whitewater River 'bootleg' camp on the early morning of Monday, December 30, 1929. That same "faithful enforcement" brought Herman face to face with the shooting suspect, James Anderson, along the Lawrenceburg-Brookville Road near Longenecker Station still later that same morning. As the wind blew open his coat revealing his badge, that same "faithfulness to his sworn duty" brought Herman to empty his revolver in response to the menacing shooter standing in front of him. There are plenty of facts placing James Anderson as the shooter, the killer of Herman Lange. The only fact needed to convict the killer is the "dying declaration" of the sheriff "faithful to his duty." Judge Lowe pleads to the jury to follow this fact to its logical conclusion and bring justice for the family, the friends, the citizens of Dearborn County in their loss of Sheriff Herman Lange. Lowe finishes. Handkerchiefs dab at the corners of each and every eye in the room.

The jury takes the case into their hands. They will decide the fate of Sheriff Herman Lange's killer. Records of Franklin County Circuit Court's Thirty-sixth Day of the April Term, June 7, 1930 show the following:

STATE OF INDIANA VS. JAMES ANDERSON No. 2018
First Degree Murder,
TRIAL ENTRY FOR TWELFTH DAY INCLUDING
JUDGMENT OF VERDICT OF JURY

Comes now the State of Indiana by counsel as of yesterday, and comes also the defendant herein in person and in the custody of Elmer Personett, Sheriff of Franklin County, Indiana, and by counsel as of yesterday, and comes also the jury heretofore duly and legally empanelled and sworn to well and truly try the issues joined herein, and being the same jury as of yesterday, and now counsel for the State of Indiana and the defendant herein present their closing arguments to such jury, and the hearing of the argument of counsel herein is completed.

And the defendant herein having heretofore on yesterday tendered to the Court his written Requested Instruction No. 1 together with a written request for the giving thereof to the jury in this cause, the court at this time now refuses to give such instruction, to which action of the court the defendant at the time expressly objects and excepts.

And the State of Indiana Herein having heretofore on yesterday tendered to the Court its written Requested Instructions numbered 1, 2, 3, 4, 5, 6, 7, 8, 9, 10, 11, 12, 13, 14, 15, 16, 17, 18, 19, 20, 21, 22, 23, 24, 25, 26, 27, and 28 together with a written request for the giving thereof to the jury in this cause, the Court at this time refuses to give Requested Instructions of the State of Indiana numbered 1, 2, 3, 4, 5, 6, 7, 8, 9, 10, 14, 17, 18, 19, 20, 21, 22, 23, 24, 25, 26, 27 and 28 and each of them, to which action of the court the State of Indiana at the time expressly objects and excepts as to each of such instructions so refused, separately and severally, and such objections and exceptions are now reduced to writing and endorsed upon such tendered Requested Instructions. And now, the argument having been concluded, the court instructs the jury herein in writing, giving of the Court's own motion, written instructions numbered 1, 2, 3, 4, 5, 6, 7, 8, 9, 10, 11, 12, 13, 14, 15, 16, 17, 18, 19, 20, 21, 22, 23, 24, 25, 26, 27, 28, 29, 30, 31, 32, 33, 34, 35, 36, 37, 37 ½, 38, 39, 40 ,41, 42, 43, 44 ,45, 46, 47, 48 and 49, which are all of the instructions given by the court to the jury herein. And now at this time the State of Indiana and the defendant herein by their respective counsel expressly object and except to the action of the court in giving to the jury of the court's own motion each and every one of such instructions so given to the jury, separately and severally as to each instruction and separately and severally as to the State of Indiana and the defendant herein, and the State of Indiana at this time further reduces to writing endorsed upon such written instructions so given its objections and exceptions, and the defendant at this time further reduces to writing endorsed upon such written instructions so given his objections and exceptions as to such written instructions so given, and as to the refusal to give Defendant's Requested Instruction Number 1 herein.

And comes now the Court in open court and files with the Clerk of his Court in open Court the requested instructions of the State of Indiana herein above numbered, Together with the written objections and exceptions endorsed thereon, and the requested instruction of the defendant herein numbered 1, and the instructions given to the jury of the court's own motion, together with the written objections and exceptions of the State of Indiana and of the defendant herein endorsed thereon, including defendant's objections and exceptions with reference to refusal to give his tendered instruction Number 1, all of which read as follows, to-wit: (H.I.).[51]

---

[51] *State of Indiana vs. James Anderson, No. 2018*, Franklin County Circuit Court, 07 June 193

The objection to instruction 1 by the defense comes from the admission of the "dying declaration" by the judge. "The competency of this evidence (dying declarations) is a question for the trial court to determine by the proof relative to the declarant's state of mind at the time he made the declarations…Proof of the fact thus to be settled by the judge is not limited to the declarant's statement alone, but it may be inferred from the general statements, conduct, manner, symptoms, and condition of the declaring, which flow as the reasonable and natural results from the extent and character of his wound, or the state of his illness."[52]

Herman's signed statement was made just a few hours (signed at 4:00 P.M.….died at 10:50 P.M.) before his death. His suffering had been intense since the time he was shot. He underwent a serious operation and he was apparently conscious of his condition. He realized he was near death and stated the same. Not only at the time he signed the "dying declaration" did he think he was going to die, but immediately after he was shot he felt the same. He stated to Emma Maines at that time that, "that was going to kill me, and I won't get over it."

Considering all the facts and the nature of Herman's wounds the court is warranted in the belief that the "dying declaration" was made with a sense of impending death without hope of recovery. Emma Maines' testimony corroborates the declaration made later. Because of these facts, the court's instructions to the jury stand.

Judge O'Byrne does his due diligence to the defense claim of self-defense. He explains to the jury that if they believe Anderson shot in self-defense, they cannot return a

---

[52] *Williams vs. State,* 1924, 196 Ind. 84, 147 N. E. 153, "The court, speaking by Myers, J."

guilty verdict on the indictment as presented.

The jury, having its instructions, deliberates the case for three and one-half hours. Their duty being performed, they return to the court room.

It is late in the day and everyone is tired. A busy hum like a thousand bees hangs over the courtroom. The judge pounds his gavel and the crowd falls silent. It has been a long wait of better than five months for Mayme, Stella, and all of Dearborn County. They could sense vindication and closure as the Judge asks the jury's foreman for their decision. The crowd hangs on every word like a congregation to their preacher at the pulpit. Foreman George Brackney announces the verdict.

And now comes such jury in open court and returns a verdict herein into open court, which verdict reads as follows, to wit:

STATE OF INDIANA VS. JAMES ANDERSON No. 2018
VERDICT

We, the jury, find the defendant, James Anderson, guilty of murder in the first degree, as charged in the indictment herein.

George Brackney, Foreman[53]

The standing room only crowd erupts in a frenzy.

Judge Roscoe C. O'Byrne prepares to hand James Anderson his sentence. The Judge asks the defendant if he has anything to say before the sentence is pronounced.

James Anderson, face like a blank piece of paper, replies, "I have nothing to say."

The audience in the overflowing courtroom buzzes with excitement about the outcome of the swift path to judgment for this case. Mayme and Stella are relieved. Their long, tiresome

---

[53] *State of Indiana vs. James Anderson, No. 2018,* Franklin County Circuit Court, 07 June 1930

journey to closure appears to be ended. With the judge's sentence they can move on with their life without Herman. Judge O'Byrne next pronounces the judgment.

STATE OF INDIANA VS. JAMES ANDERSON No. 2018

Crime- First Degree Murder

JUDGMENT ON VERDICT JURY AUTHORIZING DEATH PENALTY

Comes now the State of Indiana by Julius G Schwing, Prosecuting Attorney within and for the Thirty Seventh Judicial Circuit of Indiana, of which Judicial Circuit Dearborn County forms a part, and by Charles A. Lowe, heretofore appointed by the Dearborn Circuit Court of Indiana as Assistant Counsel for the State, and by Charles R. Baker, Prosecuting Attorney within and for the Thirty Seventh Judicial Circuit of Indiana, of which Judicial Circuit Franklin County forms a part, and by Crawford A. Peters, Assistant Counsel for the State, and comes also the defendant herein in person, and by C. W. Napier and William L. Chambers, his attorneys, and in the custody of Elmer Personett, Sheriff of Franklin County, Indiana, and the Court finds that the defendant, James Anderson, is twenty-one (21) years of age, and that said defendant is guilty of the crime charged in the indictment herein, namely: Murder in the first degree.

IT IS BY THE COURT THEREFORE ORDERED AND ADJUDGED that the said defendant for the offense by him committed do suffer death; that such punishment of death shall be inflicted by causing to pass through the body of the defendant a current of electricity of sufficient intensity to cause death, and the application and continuance of such current through his body of such defendant until such defendant be dead; that such penalty shall be inflicted before the hour of sunrise on Wednesday, the first day of October, 1930 by the Warden of the Indiana State Prison at Michigan City, Indiana, or such other official as may be authorized by law to serve as executioner in his stead and that such penalty shall be inflicted inside the walls of the Indiana State Prison at Michigan City, Indiana, in such room as may at that time be provided therefore.

IT IS FURTHER ORDERED AND ADJUDGED BY THE COURT that this judgment shall be held and construed to be full and sufficient authority for the doing and performance of any and all acts and things on the part of the Sheriff of Franklin County, Indiana and the Warden of the Indiana State Prison at Michigan City, Indiana that may be requisite for the carrying hereof into execution.

The Sheriff of Franklin County, Indiana, and the Warden of the Indiana State Prison at Michigan City, Indiana are charged with the execution of the above and foregoing judgment.[54]

Anderson displayed no emotion, blank-faced like a corpse in his coffin, when the jury returned its verdict. He, likewise, shows none at the sentence by Judge O'Byrne. The defendant's father, Isiah Anderson, who had been at James' side during the entire trial, stands as the lone relative present when the sentence is read.

Court is about to be adjourned with one final piece of business to be completed in the Anderson Case. Sentence has been passed. Where will James Anderson be held?

STATE OF INDIANA VS JAMES ANDERSON No. 2018
First Degree Murder

---

[54] *State of Indiana vs. James Anderson, No. 2018,* Franklin County Circuit Court, 07 June 1930

ORDER DEFENDANT'S TRANSFER TO UNION COUNTY

Now on this date, and after the pronouncement of judgment and sentence herein, it appears to the satisfaction of the Court that the ends of justice would be better sub served, and peace and quietude in the County of Franklin, and State of Indiana, would be furthered, by the immediate transfer of the defendant herein, James Anderson, from the County Jail of Franklin County, Indiana to the County Jail of Union County, Indiana, at Liberty, Indiana.[55]

James Anderson Prisoner Number 13954

---

[55] *State of Indiana vs. James Anderson, No. 2018,* Franklin County Circuit Court, 07 June 1930

Sheriff Personett of Franklin County fears that an attempt on Anderson's life may be made. He removes the prisoner to the Union County jail immediately following the sentence.

Upon his arrival at the Liberty, Indiana jail, James Anderson has some somber words for his new custodian, Sheriff Ellison of Union County. Anderson says to Ellison, "It isn't having to die that is so terrible but it's the hundred days I have to wait and think about it."

A hundred and fifty-nine days passed since Herman was shot performing his duty early morning, December 30, 1929. Justice has been served. Mayme resumes her duties as Sheriff of Dearborn County. Stella Mae prepares for her junior year at Lawrenceburg High School. James Anderson takes up residence on Death Row at the Michigan City Indiana State Prison.

Michigan City Indiana State Prison

~

Just like that it is over. I can open my eyes. I have waited for this moment. I believe that this conclusion should return my life right back to where it was. Like the actors on the movie screen at the Walnut Theatre, I should walk out and live happily ever after. Somehow I don't feel like that.

I watch as Mom talks to all the people standing around her in the courtroom. I hear her talk about what will happen next to Anderson. I hear her talk about Seiter and Bradburn still in her jail. I hear her talk about what will happen next for the camps along the Whitewater River. Her conversations don't sound like "riding off in the sunset." Instead, I hear "we still have a lot of work to do."

After twelve days of trial, I feel no better than I did when it began.

28

"Motions, Appeals and Stays"

People say I should be pleased that my Dad's killer has been brought to justice. I don't know. I feel no relief. I feel only emptiness.

Stella Mae Lange – *My Journal, 06/08/1930*

We went to the Trinity Lutheran Church with Suzie and Millie this morning in Klemmes Corner. Trial is over. School is out. We're home again. I can't wait to see Ginny. We haven't talked for weeks. We have a lot of things to do this summer. If I can get my head cleared of all the trial stuff, I'll be ready for a grand time.

Mom has a lot of catching up on all the record keeping and accounting for the jail. She sat down at her desk Monday morning and she didn't take her nose out of her ledgers until supper. Tuesday she's taking me downtown shopping for a new summer dress. Ginny's going too.

Mom says little about the trial all week. She doesn't appear to be pleased with the outcome. I don't sense the relief of tension that I had expected to see in her. Finally with the arrival of the newspaper, Mom sits down to share what she has read. The Thursday, June 12, edition of *The Lawrenceburg*

Press tells a brief story of the trial just completed. More ominously, this report portends things to come. The people of Dearborn County, Mom, and I all believe our journey to justice is over. Is it?

~

Anderson Is Given Penalty of Death For the Slaying of Sheriff Lange December 30th Last, At Conclusion of Brookville Trial
OCTOBER 1 EXECUTION DATE
Unless granted a new trial, provocative of a change in verdict by the supreme court of the state of Indiana, James Anderson, slayer of Sheriff Herman Lange of Dearborn County, will expiate his crime in the electric chair at Michigan City before sunrise on the morning of October 1st next. Anderson, 21, came to Indiana from Hazard, Kentucky, for some time made his home near Brookville.

Anderson was convicted of first degree murder by a jury in circuit court at Brookville. Judge Roscoe C. O'Byrne presiding, on Saturday night last at 8 o'clock, and immediately the prisoner at the bar was sentenced to death in the electric chair. Trial of Anderson ended the last day of court, hence the immediate pronouncement of the penalty by the trial judge.

C. W. Napier, attorney for the defendant, has given notice that he will ask for a new trial, which if denied, an appeal will be taken.

The crime was committed in Dearborn County taken to Franklin on a change of venue.[56]

~

---

[56] *The Lawrenceburg Press,* 12 June 1930, 1

What a jolt. This report of a possible new trial really blows heavy storm clouds over my thoughts of a good time summer. Mom's red face and puffy eyes tell me she has been crying. Dinner is quick and quiet. I am supposed to meet Ginny tonight. I'll call her after supper and beg out. I'm not ready to go through this again.

~

On Saturday, June 21, James Anderson is taken to the state penitentiary at Michigan City to begin his stay on Death Row. Deputy Sheriff James Hulbert of Dearborn County and Sheriff Elmer Personett of Franklin County deliver the inmate to his new home.

Charles Napier, attorney for Anderson, files his motion and grounds for a new trial with the Franklin County Court on June 28. On July 5, he files his affidavit in this case supporting his motion for dismissal.

~

July 6 is my birthday. I turn sixteen. This is not the sixteenth birthday I anticipated. Other kids have a nice cake. They have lots of candles. They have a dazzling party dress. Some are off with a young man riding in an automobile down the streets of Lawrenceburg. What about my joy on this happy occasion? What are my rights? Some scruffy looking hooligan shoots Dad and I have to suffer because of it? I feel terrible and I don't know how to change that.

Mom does realize my birthday is ruined. She grabs her

purse and my hand and whisks me off to the Walnut Theatre. Unfortunately, not even the popcorn can rescue this night. The Marx Brothers in *Animal Crackers* turns out to be far from humorous.

On July 7, Napier files his motion for a new trial. The court agrees to hear the motion when it reconvenes in September. I'll return to class then and the storm clouds will blow in all over again.

~

With the court back in session and affidavits being filed by both the state and the defendant, the ruling on the motion for a new trial moves forward. The defense disagrees with several points. From the opening of the trial Napier and Chambers argued with the correctness of the indictment. Mayme and Stella hope that Judge Roscoe C. O'Byrne was right in his guidance of this case. The battle begins. Mayme travels to the hearings with Judge Lowe. Stella stays home.

The defense fights for a charge of self-defense for defendant, James Anderson. The defendant claims that he did not know the man he encountered on the road to Brookville was the sheriff. Believing that Herman drew his gun first, the defendant thinks he could use force to repel this attack. Under criminal law Anderson needs to prove that the self-defense was justified. It would be difficult to prove self-defense with the bullet entering Herman's body just two inches below the badge. There was no hole in Herman's coat, indicating that the coat was open as his "dying declaration" indicated. The Judge did instruct the jury as to the law of self-defense.

Judge O'Byrne issued the following statement to the jury

in writing, "If after considering all the evidence, you have a reasonable doubt as to whether the defendant acted in self-defense, then he cannot be convicted."

The jury was not misled with these instructions and understood their merit in the case.

Attorneys for the defense argue against the admissibility of Herman's "dying declaration." Without the "dying declaration" there is little evidence with which to convict James Anderson. A "dying declaration" is admissible under Federal Rules of Evidence if the following facts can be established. The declarant must be unavailable. The declaration is offered in a criminal prosecution for homicide. The statement is made with the declarant under the belief that his death is imminent. The declarant's statement relates to the cause of what he believes to be his impending death. In the trial Judge O'Byrne allowed Herman's statement to be used as evidence. Likewise, in the motion for a retrial, the judge reaffirmed the reliability of the "dying declaration" and upheld it as acceptable evidence.

The sheriff's signed statement was made several hours before his death. From the time he was shot, his suffering was intense. He had been operated upon and was apparently conscious of his condition. He realized death was near and so stated. Not only did Herman believe he was going to die when he signed the statement; but immediately after he was shot, he told Emma Maines that this was going 'to kill him and he wouldn't get over it.' The trial court warranted in the belief that the declarations were made under a sense of impending death, without hope of recovery and the admission of the statement was correct.

The defense offers the admission of testimony of

Anderson's companions, Gus Seiter and Roscoe Bradburn as a reason crying for retrial. They said that they were with Anderson the night of December 29 and the morning of December 30. The three of them were riding in an automobile on the afternoon of December 29. Later that evening they visited two camps, the "Barn" and "Spikes". They had all been drinking and had some trouble at each camp. They said that James had been put out at "Spike's Camp" and as he left he turned and shot through the door, injuring Benjamin Shaw. Seiter and Bradburn were held at the "Camp" until Herman and Lafe Perpington arrived. They were arrested and taken to Lawrenceburg Jail. The evidence of Seiter and Bradburn was introduced in order to show that a felony had been committed and there was good reason for the sheriff to be on the road searching for James Anderson. Herman, in the proper discharge of the duties of his office, was pursuing Anderson, who had fled, in order to arrest him.

It was also proper to show that Anderson shot Shaw in order to show the motive and intent James had in shooting Herman. Anderson appeared at the camps with a thirty-eight revolver. He shot Shaw and then fled. He left his friends Seiter and Bradburn and was fleeing the scene of his crime. He knew that officers would pursue him. It cannot be doubted that when he met the sheriff, he was ready to shoot anyone who would attempt to arrest him. Herman's dying statement was "the wind must have blown my coat back, and when he saw my badge he shot me."

The physical facts show that Anderson barely missed the badge, and that he was shooting to kill. The circuit court committed no error in admitting the evidence of the defendant's companions. Their testimony was allowed.

Another big piece of the defendant's request for a retrial follows the court's evidentiary admission of the confession of James Anderson. Before the jury was even chosen in the trial Napier and Chambers demanded that the indictment be quashed. They said that the defendant's signed confession was made under duress. A retracing of steps from Anderson's capture to the time of his confession would confirm that the court was correct in introducing the written confession in evidence.

After shooting Herman, James Anderson fled to Connersville and then Kentucky. He remained in Kentucky for some time before he was arrested and returned to Indiana. He was first taken to Versailles where he contends he was put in fear. He claims that those present made threats against him and treated him roughly. He also said that there was a large crowd present, and he was afraid they would "string him up." Those present at Versailles swore that Anderson was treated kindly and that he was not scared. They said that he was not put in fear by those present. The court rules that the defendant was treated fairly and with consideration in the Ripley County Jail at Versailles.

From Versailles Anderson was moved to the Greensburg Jail in Decatur County. It was at this jail that Anderson told officials that he wished to make a confession. James requested to make his confession shortly after he had been allowed to attend a Baptist Church service in Greensburg. It was at this service that he confessed his guilt, atoned for his sin, and was baptized. Surely Anderson's penitent church experience more accounted for his willingness to confess than did any "supposed" coercion at the jail. Those present at the confession were Judge Lowe, Assistant Prosecutor, Ora Slater, Cal Crim

Detective, Julius Schwing, Prosecuting Attorney, Newt Coy, Sheriff of Decatur County, James Holbert, Deputy Sheriff of Dearborn County.

Anderson was brought in to meet those who were present to hear his confession. He began to speak before he even sat down. Julius Schwing told Anderson that he didn't have to talk unless he wished to do so. One of those present testified that Anderson acted normally and wanted to tell his story as he now had 'religion.' Evidence shows the defendant was told he had the right to counsel to advise him. He was also told that if he made a confession, it might be used against him.

Anderson responsed, "What was good enough to live by was good enough to die by." Defense contends the confession was secured by coercion, promises, and threats. Evidence, other than that of the defendant, shows no elements of coercion or threats. One of those present at Versailles, Dr. Jackson, urged the defendant to tell the truth. Deputy Sheriff Holbert told Anderson that making a confession "would save him some time." The court ruled that these statements showed no promise, coercion, threats. There was no evidence of the confession being given under duress.

On Monday morning, September 8, 1930, less than a month before James Anderson was sentenced to die, Judge Roscoe C. O'Byrne of the Franklin County Circuit Court make the following ruling on the defendant's motion for a retrial.

STATE OF INDIANA VS JAMES ANDERSON
MOTION FOR NEW TRIAL DENIED.

The court duly and sufficiently advised in the premises, now overrules and denies such motion for a new trial of this proceeding, to which action of the court, the defendant at the time expressly objects and excepts, and now overrules and denies such supplemental motion for a new trial hereof, to which action of the court the defendant at the time expressly objects and excepts. And the defendant herein by counsel, now following such actions of the court herein serves upon the counsel for the State of Indiana herein as herein above mentioned, and upon Henry J. Meyer, as Clerk of the Franklin Circuit Court of Indiana, the written notice of the defendant's intention to appeal the above entitled cause to the Supreme Court of the State of Indiana, which written notices, together with the acknowledgement of service thereof, on the part of both counsel for the State of Indiana and Henry J. Meyer, as Clerk of the Franklin Circuit Court.[57]

In all arguments of the defense for a retrial, the Circuit Court of Franklin County under Judge Roscoe C. O'Byrne denies the request for retrial. The attorneys for the defense prepare to appeal the case to the Indiana Supreme Court.

~

I used to love to listen to tales of broken hearts and triumphs and the odd twists of life. But my own story has taken over the part of me that was open to such things. I now begin my junior year at Lawrenceburg High with still no closure of the trial of James Anderson, my Father's murderer. Here we go again. I should be enjoying Lawrenceburg's basketball games with Ginny, but I'm battered with more trial garbage.

~

---

[57] *State of Indiana vs. James Anderson, No. 2018,* Franklin County Circuit Court, 08 September 1930

On February 28, 1931 the process of appeal to the Indiana Supreme Court begins with an order for the transcript delivery of case number 2018 from the 37th Judicial Circuit of Indiana in Franklin County. The order demands the court shorthand stenographer transcribe the trial shorthand records into long hand. The Treasury of Dearborn County must pay for the transcript since James Anderson is unable to pay. With this record of case 2018 in hand, Attorneys C. W. Napier, William L. Chambers, and Tremain and Turner formulate an appeal to Indiana's highest court. Before the Supreme Court, Anderson's attorneys argue that the lower Court erred in overruling the motion for a new trial. The defense attorneys say the sheriff's "dying declaration" should not be allowed. The defense claims that Anderson's signed confession was taken under coercion with threats and promises being made. They also declare that Anderson's companions, Gus Seiter and Roscoe Bradburn, should not be allowed to present evidence as witnesses. Finally, they claim that the jury was not properly instructed as to the possibility of self-defense. The Indiana Supreme Court rules against each of these claims and offers no hope for a retrial to Anderson's attorneys.

~

Through every motion, hearing, and stay the people of Dearborn County, Mom, and I anxiously await the decisions. The heart wrenching days of trial at Brookville, of appeal, of Supreme Court consideration never produce closure. The verdict declared that should have soothed our broken hearts instead turned into weeks and months of waiting for finality. There will be no healing for us.

29

"Mayme and Stella Move On"

I love school. Moving to a new school in Lawrenceburg is a joy. I get good grades. I really love choir. Graduation is a sentimental tug at my heart. Mom excites me with the promise of trips to Florida, Chicago and Iowa .What a bright new summer it is.

Stella Mae Lange – *My Journal, 05/25/1932*

Having suffered through the trial's slow march to bring justice, Mom is more than ready to get on with her life. She still has the remaining months of 1930 to fulfill her obligations to Dearborn County as their sheriff. She works hard to be a good servant. The Sheriff's Arrest Log shows her name peppering the pages of the book, as she makes numerous arrests throughout her remaining months as sheriff.

As September of 1930 unfolds, Mom takes painful time from her duties as sheriff to campaign. She brags of spending only forty-seven dollars in finance of her campaign. She still handily wins the 1930 election for a four year term as Dearborn's County Recorder. Her usually detailed and exact record keeping explain her expense

Mayme's 1930 Campaign Expenses

Giving up her seat as Sheriff in January, 1931, Mom finds a house and moves us across from the jail to a small white frame house at 311 West High Street. She says the property is reasonably priced. It is conveniently located near Mom's work as recorder and my studies at Lawrenceburg High School. What we don't count on are the memories the sight of the jailhouse evokes as we walk out our front door. The memories of Dad's year as sheriff and of Mom's year as sheriff are bittersweet. They are a reminder of the good and the sorrowful of our life shared.

In moving permanently to Lawrenceburg, Mom

continues to rent our seventy-one acre farm in Wrights Corner. Mom and I were always happy on that farm. With the farm gone and Dad gone, we can never regain that feeling. I wish we could return to that farm. I know with Dad gone and Mom working we could not handle the chores of the farm.

Mayme and Stella at House on 311 West High Street

Mom begins her job as County Recorder in January, 1931. I am so glad to be done with the jail house. The county recorder's massive red binders show evidence of Mom's hand throughout the books. Foreclosures, transfers, sales of property in this time of the Great Depression lace the impoverished county. Mom oversees it all. She prepared well for this undertaking with her time spent helping Dad in record keeping administration for the sheriff's department.

Mayme Lange at County Recorder's Desk

Mom must attend to our financial security. Mom shares with me Court documents she files seeking my guardianship. She records the sale of much of Dad's belongings. The proceeds of this sale will be placed in the trust she opens to provide for me when I reach the age of twenty-one. Life on the farm taught us to be self-sufficient. The Daughters of America offer Mom help providing for me, but she turns them down.

With all the accuracy and discipline of a skilled book-keeper, Mom puts her pen in hand and details a ledger of all credits and expenses necessary for the guardianship trust she arranges for my care. The formal court records and hand written financial accountings show no tear stains. Mom is always totally serious. She makes no show of her true feelings. Her Lutheran upbringing allows no display of grief. She attends to the business of life. I wish I could be as hardened to grief as Mom.

Stella Lange 1932 Graduating Lawrenceburg High School

I finish my schooling at Lawrenceburg High School in May, 1932. I have always been a very good student, and I have always been on the honor roll. Mom approves of my efforts. I am glad she loves my work. There was one painful and decisive drop in my grades for the one quarter immediately following Dad's death. I put the painful trial and appeals behind me and refocused on my studies. I enjoy Reading and Math, but I don't think I have Mom's knack for organization and figures. Choral group offers the comfort of escape. I love to sing. School keeps me busy and helps me avoid the mourning and distraction of Dad's loss.

I will graduate from Lawrenceburg in June, 1932. Mom is so happy I will finish. She steps out of character taking me on a midweek afternoon trip to Neff's Department Store in Aurora. "The only business we must attend to today is what dress will show you off as the belle of the class of '32." I never knew Mom to have a frivolous bone in her body. The navy, mid-length, drop-waist dress with a creamy white lace collar convinces me that—as Mom suggests—that graduation may be a grand day after all.

School finished, Mom and I take time to escape from Lawrenceburg. After graduation Mom loads up the Hupmobile and drives us to Florida. This will be a huge trip. All of our years on the farm we never went anywhere for vacation. Mom talks about this journey all year. Letters go back and forth between Mom and Aunty Betty planning the trip. Now we are on the road. We stop in the Smokey Mountains and for a night in Georgia. Other than those stops we motor straight to Miami.

Upon arriving, we find Betty waiting on her front porch for us. We are dead tired, but after unpacking our things we stay up all night talking to Betty. I forgot that Betty sings so well. Mom says I get my love of music from the Gesells. I don't know if that's true, but I sure wish I could sing as well as Betty. I can sit here and listen to her all night.

On our first day in Miami, Betty takes us to the beach. I

have never experienced anything like the white smooth sand squishing through my toes or the azure blue waves rolling over my knees and pushing me down into the water. Maybe I should ask Mom if I can come live with Betty. I broach the subject and the two sisters laugh at my foolish notion. I don't think it's a notion. I would really like to stay. Days on the beach, afternoons shopping, evenings dining all too soon come to an end. We say our good-byes and head back north to Lawrenceburg and reality.

Miami isn't our only vacation. In the summer of 1933, we take off on another road trip .This time the Chicago World's Fair promises adventure and escape for Mom and me. We load the sedan and follow the roads to the Windy City. We spend a glorious five days exploring the wonders of the Exposition along the shore of Lake Michigan. I hope Mom and I can travel like this every year.

~

I will make one more trip west this summer of 1933. With several stays for James Anderson in 1933 due to his soon to be heard appeal to the Indiana Supreme Court, Mom knows that I need a break from the agonizing wait for justice. Mom stays behind to await the outcome of the Supreme Court decision, but she boards me on a train westbound for Davenport, Iowa. Here I will visit Uncle Charles Gesell—a teacher in Davenport schools—and his sons, Cranston and Robert. I met the twins only once years ago at a Gesell Family reunion.

Mom and I get up very early for the drive to Cincinnati. My train to Davenport leaves from Union Terminal at eight a.m. We arrive early to get my ticket and find where I board. I heard a lot about this new train station, but I never realized it was so big and so grand. I could spend the day just admiring all the murals on the walls. The great rotunda is a little overwhelming and the huge crowds rattle my nerves a bit. Mom finds the ticket booth, calms me down, and steers me to my boarding area. I so want to go to Davenport, but I am reluctant to leave Mom and take off by myself. Mom goes over my route and my plans calming my nerves enough to get me aboard the train.

Once aboard, I settle into a window seat and feast my eyes on the scenery. I watch the fields, and trees, and houses reel past the car windows. It's six hours to Chicago and another three hours to Davenport, so I pull out the book I brought along and try to get comfortable in the hard upholstered train seat. I have read and enjoyed several of Carolyn Keene's *Nancy Drew Mysteries* so I am eager to dig into this new work *The Clue in the Diary.* Ginny loved it and lent me her copy for the trip. A good "whodunit" ought to prevent the click-clack of the train wheels from lulling me to sleep.

At three p.m. we stop over in Chicago. The train lays over an hour, but I stay on so as not to get lost. I thought Cincinnati was busy. Chicago's Union Station buzzes with a bee hive of activity. I have never seen so many people scurrying around. I grab a sandwich in the club car during the stop and I am soon back on the tracks to Iowa.

On the train, as the sun set, I watch the world pass by in yellow and pink sunset, fields and lakes, small houses with scrub yards, washing hung up, tall, narrow trees, lightless and struggling. We pull into Davenport's Abbey Station just about eight p.m. I recognize Uncle Charles right away. It has been so long since I saw Cranston and Robert that I hardly recognize them. They are each about a year older than me, but they look so much older and more handsome than all the boys back in Lawrenceburg. I smile and hug Charles and we take off for their farm. I am going to love this week.

We ride horse-back around the farm. It's like Wrights Corner all over only greener and sunnier and flatter. Cranston and Robert escort me to the Uptown Theatre in Davenport. We sing our way through *42ⁿᵈ Street*. I love musicals.

Iowa, what a great trip. I hope I can return to see Cranston and Robert. Alas, I have been done with school for a whole year and I seem to be going nowhere. I need to find a job and get on with my life. Talk says Prohibition will come to an end soon. Quaker is building a distillery in Lawrenceburg— once completed, there should be plenty of jobs available. Oh boy, the good news arrived today. I'm going to work at Quaker Distillery in September. With a good job maybe I can take some more fantastic trips.

30

"Sentence Commuted"

Why is Mom so troubled? She says she must go to Indianapolis to talk to the Parole Board concerning James Anderson. I thought he was out of our life. Does this ever end? She says her words can keep him on "Death Row". She's travelling with Judge Lowe to the hearings. I worry about her. For the first time I see her shaken.

Stella Mae Lange – *My Journal, 09/15/1933*

On July 1, 1933, while I was immersed in the delights of Davenport, the members of Indiana's Supreme Court ruled on the appeal for a retrial in the case of James Anderson vs. The State of Indiana.

~

Chief Justice David A. Myers and Associate Judges James P. Hughes, Michael L. Fansler, Curtis Roll, and Walter E. Treanor agree that the Franklin County Circuit Court's decision under Judge Roscoe C. O'Byrne to deny a retrial for James Anderson should be upheld. Mayme saved the court decision to share with Stella upon her return from Iowa. Can this be something that has the taste of good news?

*To Clerk of Circuit Court of d County (*Franklin*), Greeting:*

*You are hereby notified that the Supreme Court of Indiana has affirmed the judgment of the Court (Franklin) below in the above entitle case. (*James Anderson vs. State of Indiana).[58]

Before the Supreme Court, Anderson's attorneys argued that the lower Court erred in overruling the motion for a new trial. The defense attorneys said Herman's "dying declaration" should not be allowed. The defense claimed that Anderson's signed confession was taken under coercion with threats and promises being made. They also declared that Anderson's companions, Gus Seiter and Roscoe Bradburn, should not be allowed to present evidence as witnesses. Finally, they claimed that the jury was not properly instructed as to the possibility of self-defense. The Indiana Supreme Court ruled totally against each of these claims and offered no hope of a retrial for Anderson's attorneys. It sure doesn't seem final to Stella.

~

I'm not really sure what all these legal statements mean, but I'm ready to be done with all of this. Anderson did it. He should be put away. We should not live in fear of him coming after us. Through every motion, hearing, and stay Mom and I anxiously await the decisions. The heart wrenching days of trial at Brookville, of appeal, of Supreme Court consideration never produce the closure we need. The verdict that should soothe our broken hearts instead turns into weeks and months

---

[58] *State of Indiana vs. James Anderson, No. 2018,* Franklin County Circuit Court, 29 June 1933

of waiting for finality of healing. The grieving do not heal. I crawl into my grief and cocoon it around me.

~

In early December, 1933, Judge Lowe comes to see Mayme. He tells her that Defense Attorney C. W. Napier is well respected in Hazard, Kentucky as a tenacious and hardworking prosecuting attorney. Napier's bulldog like approach drives him to make appeals again and again to keep James Anderson from the electric chair. In all nine stays of execution are granted as the defense keeps pushing against the will of the courts and the people of Indiana. Even though Anderson still sits on Death Row, scheduled for execution, the judge expresses concern that the fight is not over. *The Lawrenceburg Register* details James Anderson's road from "death row" in Michigan City's Indiana State Penitentiary to something else.

Anderson's Sentence Is Commuted To Life

Governor Paul V. McNutt Wednesday December 7, 1933, commuted the sentence of James Anderson to life imprisonment in the state prison at Michigan City. Anderson was to have been executed last Friday for the murder of Sheriff Herman Lange. Pleas for the commutation were made by attorneys for Anderson, his parents and relatives.

The Governor said that he had decided to commute sentence after studying the evidence in his trial and because of his previous record.

Anderson's case attracted wide attention and it is doubtful if many persons condemned to die had more stays of execution than he who was granted nine. The following is a

194

review of the killing and the procedure in the case since then.

Anderson shot Sheriff Lange early on the morning of December 30, 1929, on the highway near Longnecker Station in Harrison Township, following a disturbance at a camp on the Whitewater River near Harrison. Lange died at Cincinnati Bethesda hospital the following night.

Following the shooting Anderson escaped and a man hunt ensued which took the posse to about all parts of Franklin county and finally to the old home of Anderson in the hills of Kentucky. The posse was unsuccessful in capturing Anderson but detective Slater started working on the case in conjunction with the officers of several counties in Kentucky.

On Tuesday morning, March 11, Anderson was arrested at Buckhorn, Kentucky by Deputies Alfred Amis and Sam Begley. Anderson was staying at the home of a relative near Buckhorn and fled when the officers approached the home but was captured after a short chase.

Anderson was returned from Kentucky on Wednesday, March 12 and taken to the jail at Versailles where he remained until the next evening when he was taken to the Greensburg jail.

On the following Saturday afternoon he made a voluntary confession at the Greensburg jail to Prosecutor Julius Schwing, Assistant Prosecutor Charles A. Lowe, Deputy James Hulbert, Detective Ora Slater, court stenographer Edgar Kurtzman and Sheriff Coy of Decatur county.

The trial of Anderson started at Brookville in the Franklin County Circuit Court on May 26 and was concluded on June 7 when the jury brought in a verdict of guilty and Anderson was sentenced to die in the electric chair at the State prison on October 1. He was then taken to the Union county jail at Liberty. On June 21 he was removed to the State prison by Deputy Sheriff Hulbert and the Sheriff of Franklin County.

On July 16, arguments were submitted before Judge Roscoe O'Byrne at Brookville upon the motion for a new trial for Anderson. Action was postponed on the matter by the Judge until the first day of the September term of court. The motion was overruled on September 5 and attorneys for Anderson appealed the case to the Indiana Supreme Court.

In the meantime he was granted a stay of execution until February 6, 1931 when he was supposed to die for his crime. Pending the appeal to the Supreme Court he was granted another stay until November 6 of the same year. Later he was given another stay until May 13, 1932, so that his lawyers might have more time to produce evidence and start proceeding for a new trial. On May 10 he was granted a further stay of execution until December 16.

On December 5, 1932 he was granted stay of execution until May 19, 1933 as an appeal from his conviction was filed with the Supreme Court. On May 15 he was given a stay until September 8 and on August 23, a stay until October 27. On October 17 a petition for another
stay was filed with the Supreme Court and granted, time for his execution to be November 24.

On Monday November 20, the Indiana Supreme Court granted another stay for Anderson until Friday December 8.

On November 23, Anderson was denied a rehearing by the Supreme Court. On the same day his father and mother and two ministers and two attorneys appeared before Governor Paul V. McNutt and asked that the death sentence be commuted to a life term.

The Governor announced that he would not rule on the

petition until attorneys for Anderson had an opportunity to obtain statements from the prosecuting attorneys and judge who tried the case. The Governor indicated that he would be guided largely by their statements.

Anderson's trial was costly to Dearborn County. Court costs paid by the county to Franklin County where he was tried were $2332.04. This does not include other costs such as mileage, reward, and other expenses.[59] (Mileage was $1320.20 and reward was $500.00).

The judge tries hard to find reasons for the governor's decision. He lays out what he can understand for Mayme to chew on. Lowe cannot digest Governor Paul V. McNutt's commutation of Anderson's sentence. The governor is a Democrat with a reputation of an old style machine politician. The Langes were Republicans. Dearborn County government and judicial offices were populated with Republicans. McNutt even postpones 1933 municipal elections for supposed financial reasons keeping the state's Democratic majority in power for another year. He does this by means of the "Skip-Election Law of 1933". He also consolidates 168 of the state's governmental agencies into just eight departments. McNutt takes control of many state agencies including the state police, the bureau of criminal investigation, the board of clemency, and the state probation department.

With McNutt going to extremes—using executive privilege to deny voting rights and to consolidate power within the executive branch—he might be tempted to commute a sentence with little or no persuasive input. There is little to indicate that the governor's commutation of Anderson's sentence carries political implications, but there is likewise

[59] *The Lawrenceburg Register, 14 December 1933, 1*

197

little to indicate his real intentions in changing the sentence.

In order to understand Governor McNutt's decision to commute James Anderson's sentence of death to life imprisonment, the judge must scrutinize the clemency process in Indiana a little more closely. The Constitution of Indiana gives the Governor the exclusive authority to grant reprieves, commutations, and pardons for all offenses. In death penalty cases, the clemency process was intended to function as a final safeguard. It was to evaluate the fair and judicious application of the penalty in context of the circumstances of the crime, the evidence, the individual perpetrator, and the severity of the penalty. The clemency process can only fulfill this critical function when it is governed by fundamental principles of justice, fairness, and mercy, and not be political in its considerations. To assist the Governor in his execution of clemency, the General Assembly created the Indiana Parole Board to make clemency recommendations.[60]

Before delving into the facts the Parole Board might consider in their presentation to the Governor for sentence commutation, should the indictment even have been one of First Degree Murder calling for the Death Penalty. Attorneys for the Defense, Napier and Chambers, asked in the very beginning of the trial State of Indiana vs. James Anderson for this indictment to be quashed. Judge O'Byrne denied this request and the trial proceeded. The trial proceeded because the facts exposed more than one of the statutory aggravating factors as being relevant to the case. The Death Penalty is imposed if any of the following factors exist. "The victim of a murder was a ...law enforcement officer, and either (a) the victim was acting in the course of duty or (b) the murder was

---

[60] *State of Indiana Constitution,* Article V, Executive, Section 17

motivated by an act the victim performed while acting in the course of duty. The defendant has committed another murder (Benjamin Shaw), at any time, regardless of whether the defendant has been convicted of that other murder." [61] All of these factors exist making the sentence of death correct if all facts are proven in court.

Once the inmate petitions for clemency, the Parole Board begins its hearing to determine how to answer the Governor. Statements from the trial judge and trial prosecuting attorney are gathered. The Board collects records, reports, and other information relevant in their consideration. The Board conducts a hearing to provide the petitioner and other interested people an opportunity to offer information regarding the petition. In making its recommendation to the Governor, the Board must consider several things. Does the offender have a prior criminal record? What is the offender's previous social history? What is the offender's age at the time of the crime? What are the attitudes and opinions of the community in which the crime was committed? What are the attitudes and opinions of the friends and relatives of the victim? What are the attitudes and opinions of the friends and relatives of the offender? Hearing everyone involved, the Board will render a final decision as to clemency. [62] The Parole Board makes recommendations. The Governor makes the clemency decision based on that. The Indiana Supreme Court states clemency is "a matter of grace and is not a right of the convicted felon."[63]

In 1933 Herman Lange is not the only Indiana law ~~enforcement official whose~~ murderer has his sentence

[61] *Indiana Code*, 35-50-2-9(b)(2006)
[62] *Indiana Code, 11-9-2-1, 11-9-2-2(b)(2), 11-9-2-3(b)(3), 11-9-1-3(a), 11-9-1-3(b)*
[63] *84Misenheimer vs. State*, 374 N. E. 2d 523, 532 (Ind. 1978)

commuted from Death to Life imprisonment. Frank Knoebel, a Madison, Indiana policeman, was shot and killed trying to apprehend a burglar in late December, 1930. This murderous attack in the small river town in Jefferson County was almost a year to the day after the Dearborn County Sheriff's death in the line of duty.

Officer Knoebel's murderer, twenty-nine year old Walter Carlin, was tried at Versailles in Ripley County, Indiana just to the west of Dearborn. On Friday, February 20, 1931, Carlin was pronounced guilty by a jury of twelve men of first degree murder. He was sentenced to Death by electrocution. He was taken to Death Row at the Michigan City Prison on March 8, 1931. Walter Carlin, prisoner number 14488, could very well have been held in a cell near James Anderson, prisoner number 13954.

Governor Paul McNutt's actions keep both men from facing death in the electric chair. Carlin, like Anderson, is denied in his appeal to the local circuit court and the Indiana Supreme Court. On April 14, 1933, the Governor commutes Walter Carlin's death sentence to one of life imprisonment. This executive order was made just eight months before James Anderson's sentence was commuted.

In their concern that a governor may exercise his clemency powers with a complete understanding of the facts involved, the Indiana legislature created the state commission on clemency in 1933. Prisoners not eligible for parole sought reductions in their sentence by filing petitions with the Clemency Commission under Indiana Law, *1933 Ind. Acts 721, Pub. L. No. 117, 4.* After the enactment of this 1933 law, Governor McNutt never failed to approve a single recommendation made by the Clemency Commission. Judge

Lowe surmises that the prisons are "busting at the seams" and the state can't afford to house all of its detainees. In the depth of the depression, there just was not enough money to keep all the prisoners behind bars. In the end the Judge and Mayme could only shake their heads saying "I don't understand. It's just not right."

Regardless of his reasoning in commuting Anderson's sentence, Paul McNutt signs the following Executive Order Number 8266 for Indiana State Prison inmate Number 13954, James Anderson on December 7, 1933.

WHEREAS, one James Anderson was convicted in the Circuit Court of Franklin County, Indiana, on June 7, 1930, charged with Murder, 1st Degree and sentenced and committed to the Indiana State Prison under sentence of Death; and

WHEREAS, the said James Anderson was granted stays of execution by the Supreme Court of the State of Indiana from September 17, 1930, at stated intervals, to December 8, 1933;

NOW, THEREFORE, I, Paul V. McNutt, Governor of the State of Indiana, by virtue of the power and authority vested in me by the Constitution and laws of said State, hereby commute the sentence given the said James Anderson from electrocution to life imprisonment. [64]

Mayme's ears burn with the fire kindled by the Judge's words. She vents her distaste for what has been done. "If the Governor is truly guided by the statements of the prosecuting attorneys and the case judge, how could he reach a conclusion so contrary? Assistant Prosecuting Attorney Charles A. Lowe worked hard to bring his old friends murderer to justice.

---

[64] Governor Paul McNutt, State of Indiana, *Executive Order #8266*, 07 December 1933

Herman was Lowe's riding bailiff in Dearborn County Circuit Court. Prosecuting Attorney Julius Schwing had worked closely with Herman during their term together. This man likewise had a keen interest in seeing justice served for his murdered associate and grieving family. Judge Roscoe C. O'Byrne, Franklin County Circuit Court Judge, had worked diligently to cover all bases in the call to justice made by his neighboring Dearborn County. Case law cited time and again that all the objections and exceptions brought against the Judge's rulings were unfounded. The Indiana Supreme Court upheld his court's decisions in all counts. Governor McNutt's intervention swept aside the hard work of all invested in *State of Indiana vs. James Anderson.*"

On December 7, 1933, Governor Paul McNutt commutes James Anderson's Death Penalty to Life Imprisonment.

~

Judge Lowe can barely lift his tired and puzzled head. He questions aloud, "Prohibition spawned the illegal camps that enticed James Anderson to drink and party and kill. The 18th amendment was repealed just two days before Anderson's sentence commutation. Did the legitimization of drinking bring forgiveness for its effect on Anderson's actions?"

The Death Penalty being swept aside for James Anderson, Mom and I wonder if the end is in fact life in prison or is there to be more to the story. We feel no certainty, thus we feel no comfort. I am dumbfounded. I don't understand. I fear that James Anderson will come for Mom or me next.

31

"What Now?"

Headlines on the front page of the newspapers today screamed "Democrats Win It All". I guess that means Mom is out of a job. What are we gonna' do?

Stella Mae Lange Fahey – *My Journal, 11/08/1934*

With Dad's murderer's sentence commuted to Life, we find it difficult to return to normalcy. Our desire for justice by Anderson's death is not to be. Life goes on and we must surrender and come to terms with the change. People tell us that Life in prison for Dad's murderer will have to do.

Mom and I will have to accept the outcome. We may outwardly accept what we cannot change, but the sorrow of losing Dad cuts deep. The disappointment of Anderson's death penalty commutation nags like a festering wound. There are new concerns of a possible parole that keep the wound open. Worry is a never healing injury. Bandages of suppression cover the wounds, they do not heal them. What lies inside of us is difficult to share. Life goes on.

Mom buries herself in her recorder's work. She is happy to have that job. Like everything she does, Mom's work is thorough and complete. I can close my eyes and see her standing in the Recorder's Office, pen in hand, putting ink to the affairs of the county. She holds that little Parker Duofold Fountain Pen tight like a hymnbook. The black, gold-trimmed pen's jewelry clasp hangs from Mom's small gold necklace, dangling at the ready for the business of the day.

I now work at the Quaker Distillery. The work is dull and uninteresting. I stand at an assembly line and label the bottles as they come past. I do not complain, however. There are a lot of people who have no jobs. Whenever Ginny and I go to the movie in Lawrenceburg on Saturday nights, we see men camped under the bridge near the railroad tracks. A few old men sit outside. They looked ruined and decrepit, the sort of men who'd soon turn into empty space. Papers say things are bad and jobs are scarce. I'm glad to have the work, even if for only a few days a week.

The February, 1934, newspapers herald a new round of political announcements for the May Primary Elections. Mom's name appears as the only one on the ballot for the Republican County Recorder's candidacy. Assured of appearing on the November ballot, Mom busies herself in her work as county recorder, allowing little time to campaign. Prior to the election, she pens this note appearing in the November 1, 1934, *Lawrenceburg Register*.

To the Voters of Dearborn County

I have not been able to see as many of you as I would have liked, owing to the duties of the office, but trust that you will give me your most loyal support on Tuesday's election.

I wish to thank all for the courteous treatment shown while calling on you. I have tried to perform my duties as Recorder to the best of my knowledge, and if re-elected or not, I will continue to do so to the end of my term.[65]

~

Some of Mayme's friends say that the Great Depression will make winning as a Republican candidate in any election, local or national, a tall order. Roosevelt is not on the ballot, but people like what he is doing. His results will certainly aid his Democratic Party. Even in small town Lawrenceburg, the big guns are coming out to fire up the populace for a Democratic push to victory. In the Thursday, October 16, 1934 edition of *The Lawrenceburg Register,* a full page announcement appears heralding a speaking engagement of Democratic Indiana Governor Paul McNutt at the Lawrenceburg High School gym.

Governor Paul V. McNutt will address the voters of Dearborn and surrounding counties…Friday evening, October 26. This will be the only appearance of the Governor in this part of the state during the campaign.

Governor McNutt's reputation as an orator is confined not only to Indiana, but is nationwide and his services are constantly in demand.

The meeting will start promptly at 8 o'clock and one of the largest crowds ever to attend a political speaking in Lawrenceburg is anticipated… All voters irrespective of party affiliation are invited to the meeting.[66]

The thought of Governor McNutt coming to her home town to speak in behalf of his powerful Democratic party posits a bitter taste in Mayme's mouth. Less than a year prior this same Governor had released Herman's killer from death row. McNutt is known to be a polished, dramatic, influential

---

[65] *The Lawrenceburg Register, 01 November, 1934*
[66] *The Lawrenceburg Register, 18 October, 1934*

speaker. Mayme imagines his appearance in her backyard to be a personal attack. She fears the loss of her office and livelihood.

A lot of people around town think Mayme is helpless against the Democratic juggernaut even at her local county level. They say in his last State of the Union address of December, 1928, Calvin Coolidge had declared, "The country can regard the present with satisfaction and anticipate the future with optimism."[67] Herbert Hoover travelled this road of enthusiasm to a record margin of victory in 1928. The stock market crash exploded this bubble of optimism in October of 1929. Herman rode Herbert Hoover's coattails into his office in 1928. Mayme may not be as lucky. Even though she is popular with the voters of Dearborn County, she may fight a losing battle with any Democratic candidate.

The front page headlines of *The Lawrenceburg Register* shout out the depressing news in the days following the election.

DEARBORN COUNTY APPROVES NEW DEAL!
Gains Made in State and Nation in Democratic Landslide
ENTIRE COUNTY TICKET (Democratic) IS ELECTED[68]

Just like the people in the breadlines, Mayme is out of a job. She garners more votes than any of her fellow Dearborn Republican candidates, but this is of little consolation.

~

It's 1935. The Great Depression drags the country down, leaving a third of workers unemployed. Mom ponders our

---

[67] Bill Bryson, *One Summer, America, 1927,*(Doubleday, 2013), 429
[68] *The Lawrenceburg Register, 08 November, 1934*

future .

She goes to work at Seagram's Distillery in Lawrenceburg. Like me, Mom works in the industry that prospers with the end of Prohibition. The evils of Prohibition took Dad from us. The good of Prohibition's Repeal brings us our daily bread. Life goes on.

32

"The '37 Flood"

Mom and I made it out of our house before the levee collapsed. We had help moving furniture and a few things up the hill to Grandma Lange's house in Greendale. I have been helping the Red Cross some at Seagram's, but I am afraid I might catch something.

Stella Mae Lange Fahey – *My Journal, 02/03/1937*

Life moves on for Mom and me. I meet someone who could change my life. Walking along Walnut Street in downtown Lawrenceburg on a breezy spring evening, I see Bill Fahey. He drives through town in his father's Ford. He sees me walking down the street. He turns around at the corner. He stops to ask me where I am headed. Ginny is with me when Bill stops.

She says, "That's it for you, girl." She sees the look in my eyes and knows I am in love. Of course I am. What's not to love about Bill's six foot slender frame topped by coal black hair and dark piercing "Valentino" eyes? He wears a white shirt, rolled up at the sleeves with white suspenders holding up his dark flannel pants. His rugged good looks betray his youth.

Over the summer and early fall, Bill and I see each other

every chance we get. He visits three or four times a week. If he can't get his Dad's old Ford, he finds a ride with one of his friends. Usually, Bill's friend Benny Turner brings him to town. Ginny takes a liking to Benny and we all go out together quite often. Seeing Bill alone highlights my week. We go to a movie once a week. Mom prepares dinner for us all on Sundays. Often, we just walk around Lawrenceburg planning our future together. Always dreaming of Bill, I find the weight of Dad's death to be not so heavy. I sometime think Bill helps drive the dark clouds from Mom's mournful existence. She really seems to like him.

We hope to marry early in 1937. The Ohio River flood of 1937 buries our marriage plans just like its muddy waters bury Lawrenceburg and Aurora. During the flood we are pushed apart by the rapidly rising waters between Lawrenceburg and Aurora. We communicate by mail.

~

On the grey overcast day, January 2, 1937, the clouds open over the small adjacent southeastern Indiana river towns of Lawrenceburg and Aurora. The drenching rains and the melting snows soak the low lying cities like a great wet sponge dipped and wrung for twenty-six days. The rain fell in sheets and gushes, water flung at the windows as if from a bucket. The great Ohio River erupts out of its banks spewing water across the cities like the lava flow of a fierce volcano and reaches a towering height of 82 feet on Monday, January 25. A great mass of water and floating destruction build a barrier between the drowning towns of Aurora and Lawrenceburg.

Bill, a young man of 19, lives in the small town of

Aurora with his parents and three siblings in a large frame house backing up to a river fed creek. Just upstream in Lawrenceburg, Stella, a slim brown haired girl of 22 lives with her mother in a small white house whose yard butts up to the levee holding back the mighty Ohio. The couple,dating for more than a year watch the rising waters seep into their lives.

Letters they write during their separation tell Bill and Stella's story.

Stella's '37 Flood Letter to Bill

Bill's '37 Flood Letter to Stella

Thursday, January 21, 1937
Dearest Stella Mae

Well, honey, things look bad. As I am writing this the water is still rising. It is now 64 1/2 feet high. In just a little while we will have to move upstairs. Darling, if you are still in your house you need to get out. I'm terribly afraid the levee will break. They say it is leaking now. The water is almost as high now as the last time it broke. I'm worried about you. I can't get to you because Tanner's Creek and Wilson Creek Bridges are closed. I worked with Leo this morning. The water is just about up to the Bank corner on Second Street. We are moving groceries and everything up to the second floor of the Kroger Store. Well dearest, I have to close. I miss you.

Love, Bill

~

On Tuesday, January 26, the levee has broken. Neither city has gas, electric or water. The flooding water level has risen almost 20 more feet in five days. There has been no mail in or out of Aurora, but Bill writes to his love in Lawrenceburg.

Tuesday, January 26, 1937

Dearest Stella Mae,

I hope you and your mother got out safely. We have no light, gas, or water here. Luckily we have several gallons of coal oil, a couple of lamps, and a coal oil stove. We have a little food I was able to get from Uncle Leo's store before it went under. The water pushes up to the Feed Mill on Third Street. Only Fifth Street and Sunnyside on the hill are not under water. We moved to VonLuerhte's on Fifth Street after the water overtook the second floor of our house. We got out by row boat and Dad fell in the water climbing into the boat. He is fine, just a little embarrassed. Some people don't even have a house anymore. It is impossible to get out of Aurora. The city is under military control. I will get to you.

Love, Bill

~

Bill pens another letter to Stella.

Monday, February 1, 1937

Dearest Stella Mae,

I'm getting lonesome for you. Water fell a little so I borrowed a boat to check on our house. We lost some things. Our toilet floated away. I was able to get into the second floor and clean. It will be a while before anyone can get into the first

211

floor. I was looking through a telescope at your Aunt Dora's house across town. She still has water in her second floor windows. I did get a pass from the military so I can move around town. The only way out of Aurora to Lawrenceburg is a 70 mile trip to Rising Sun then Milan to Guilford then Dover and into Homestead. Even if I had a car, I would not have enough gas to make that trip.

Don't know whether I will have any place to work when the water goes down. We saved all of Leo's things, but the Red Cross took everything. Even when the water subsides it will take time to restock his store. Maybe I can get a job at one of the distilleries. Mother, Danny, and Richard are sleeping downstairs at Jimmy Iron's place of Third Street. He manages the A & P Store and promised me a job as soon as he can open. Things look bleak, but I will find something.

Every night I go to bed I pray to God to keep you safe.

Yours Forever, Bill

~

Finally a letter Stella wrote on the previous Friday makes its way to the house on Fifth Street and Bill.

Friday, January 29, 1937

Dearest Bill,

Mom and I made it out of our house before the levee collapsed. We had help moving furniture and a few things up the hill to Grandma Lange's house in Greendale. I have been helping the Red Cross some at Seagram's, but I am afraid I might catch something. Someone said that water got into the fire boxes in the generator rooms at Seagram's and Schenley's. They brought in two steam locomotives and installed a steam line to operate the generators so that each house in Greendale could have one light. It's not a lot, but more than most people have.

Ginny and I go down every day to see how far the water has gone down. Ginny and I are together every afternoon, but the nights I just about die. I miss you so. Honey, write to me soon.

With all my love, Stella.

~

Bill spilled his heart onto the pages of his next letter.

Tuesday, February 2, 1937

Dearest,

If we could be together things would not be as bad as they are. It bothers me that I cannot see you. Water seems to be going down some more. I hope I can get a pass to come see you Wednesday. We have lost a lot but we still have each other. If I can find a job we can marry. Agree?

Honey, in your last letter your Mother said, "We can start out now if we want." Just what did you mean? Do you mean you and I can get married now? I would love nothing more.

Yours Always, Bill

~

Bill made it to Greendale Wednesday. He wrote that night.

Thursday, February 4, 1937

Darling,

I felt a lot better because I saw you today. If I knew I could get home that easy, I would stay later. Next time I will spend the whole day with you. There is a great deal of work to do now. The water is out of the house so I am cleaning to move back. If I can get the water out of the basement, I will start the fire in the furnace.

Love, Bill

~

Stella responded to Bill's visit.
Thursday, February 4, 1937
Bill Darling,
I hope you got home safe. I hated to see you leave. I miss you again. When can we marry? I hope you find work so we can start our life together.

With all my love, Stella

~

Bill answers.
Thursday Afternoon, February 4, 1937
Darling,
I have an offer of a job at the laundry. Harry says he will put in a good word for me. With a little money we could marry. I could get another job and you wouldn't have to work at the distillery. I can't wait to be with you. I wish I could crawl in bed beside you instead of having to sleep on a darn old sofa by myself.

Yours forever, Bill

~

Stella talked to her Mother concerning the future and wrote to Bill.

Friday, February 5, 1937

Honey,

Mom says we can start out now if we desire. She says we can live with her if our house still stands in Lawrenceburg. I can't wait to get back home to see where we will begin our married life. I miss you much.

Love, Stella

~

Bill quickly penned a response to Stella's news.

Saturday, February 6, 1937

Darling,

I love you more than anything in the world and I want to marry you. I must find a job. Gosh, honey I am getting desperate. If things don't change soon, I will break. I won't let you down, however. We will find a way.

Love, Bill

The water finally subsided. Bill and Stella's families returned to their homes. They all lost a lot. Bill went to work at Cook Foundry in Lawrenceburg. The flood destroyed records at the church and forced them to wait to be married. They were finally wed at St. Lawrence Catholic Church in Lawrenceburg on July 10, 1937. They set up housekeeping with Mrs. Lange and began their marriage of sixty-one years.

~

Bill and I start our married life living with Mom at the white frame house on High Street. Our daughters Marjorie Ann, born June 30, 1938, and Martha Louise, born January 17, 1940, each begin their lives in Mom's Lawrenceburg home. Our growing young family keeps my mind and heart far from the worry of justice served for Dad's murderer.

33

"Parole"

It's been years since Dad died. Time has not healed my aching memory. Days pass as in a normal life. I now have three daughters. They are good kids. I so wish they knew their Grandfather. Mom has been under the weather. She is coming soon to Cincinnati to see her family, especially her newest Grandchild, Elaine. I hope the upcoming parole hearings for James Anderson don't spoil her visit. We are all fearful of him being released.

Stella Mae Lange Fahey – My Journal, 09/02/1944

Bill and I have our financial heads above water. We can now search for our own place. Mom has been a great help to us, but it is really time to move. We find an apartment in Hartwell not far from Bill's job at GE. Mom comes occasionally to visit by bus from Lawrenceburg.

Our daughters Marjorie and Martha thoroughly enjoy Mom's visits to Cincinnati. I always see Mom as all business. She smiles little and laughs even less. I truly believe she misses Dad even more than I do. She is, however, always upbeat and playful with the girls. They lighten her face—their giggles lifting the corners of her mouth into a great grandma grin.

A short time later, we are finally able to find our own home. We move to a wonderful two-story, wood-shingled house on a tree-lined street in North College Hill. What a great place to raise our young family. When Mom visits, she sits at the family's upright piano in the dining room and entertains us with music for hours. I do wish Aunt Betty could join her. Betty has such a fine voice, and Margie and Martha would love to hear her sing. The girls never really know why Mom appears so quiet and melancholy. I know. Someday I will share the story with them.

World War II rages on, filling the newspapers with frightening headlines every day. I am so thankful that Bill's job at GE keeps him close by us. It is so distressing to see so many of our friends and relatives off in the midst of the war. Virginia, Bill's younger sister, sits at home crying while her husband Howard is off in the middle of the ocean on some godforsaken ship. When we visit, I offer my shoulder for her tear-stained face. Bill's younger brother Richard is still in high school, but he knows he will be in the service as soon as he graduates. Usually stoic Mom and Dad Fahey can barely contain their anxiety.

Gas rationing keeps us close to home. Mom hops on a Green Line bus, travelling to North College Hill to stay with us for days at a time. Bill pinches the ration purse strings so that we can travel to Lawrenceburg to visit her. She continues to work at Seagrams, and fills her spare time with her church group, the Daughters of America, and bookkeeping for the Dearborn County Republican Party. She says, "To stand still is to die." I don't believe that. I think that to stand still is to be lonely. I don't worry about being still. The girls fill my days and nights.

War or no war, the girls grow bigger every day. Soon I am pregnant again. I give birth to third daughter, Mary Elaine on July 6, 1943, also my birthday. What a wonderful birthday gift. This is a present more wonderful than the notice of a motion for retrial of Anderson I received when I turned sixteen.

In the summer of 1944 James Anderson comes up for parole. Once again prosecutors, judges, and Mom are called upon to attest to why Dad's murderer should be shown no mercy and remain in prison. It's been fifteen years since our memories have been brought down from the shelf, dusted off, and reopened to those pages of Dad's murder and Anderson's trial. I am a fortunate one in these parole hearings. With three young girls to parent, I am excused from the suffering of drudging up the old feelings. Mom is not ready to reopen these wounds inflicted by the loss of Dad. She resurrects the sense of duty lodged within her heart to reassert once more why her Husband's killer should not be spared from judgment. Mom draws the courage to testify to the enforcement of James Anderson's sentence. No parole for Dad's murderer is her demand.

Mom is under the weather after the parole hearing, not well enough to see her young Granddaughters. As Elaine approaches her first birthday, Mom determines to relish in the living and leave the gloom behind in Lawrenceburg.

Mom's heart and soul are in turmoil as her own September 9 birthday approaches. The tiring, sickening pressure of knowing her husband's murderer may be free weighs on her. She fears he will come after her; he will harm her or me and our family. Still not feeling well, Mom makes a bus trip to visit us on a September Sunday. The girls each run to hug Grandma. They are thrilled to see her. She embraces them, but sits quietly as I scurry to make dinner. She has Martha on her knee and Margie at her side as dinner is served. Soon after the meal she begs to be excused and heads to bed. She says she is just tired from the trip.

~

The rest of this history can be found on the front page of *The Lawrenceburg Register* edition of September 14, 1944.

Funeral services for Mrs. Mayme Lange, widow of Herman Lange, former Dearborn county sheriff, who died of a heart attack at the home of her daughter, Mrs. Stella Mae Fahey at North College Hill last Thursday evening, were held on Monday afternoon at Zion Evangelical and Reformed church. The Reverend H. M. Goetz, pastor of the church, officiated, and burial was in Greendale cemetery. She was 58 years old.

Mrs. Lange was born in Brookville, the daughter of Mr. and Mrs. Philip Gesell. In 1911 she was married to Herman Lange of this community and the couple established their home on a farm near Wright's Corner. They later moved to Lawrenceburg for a short period, and then returned to the farm where they continued to reside until 1929, when Mr. Lange was elected sheriff of Dearborn County and they moved to Lawrenceburg where she spent the remainder of her life. Mr. Lange was killed in the performance of his duties on December 30, 1929, and Mrs. Lange was appointed sheriff for one year to fill out his unexpired term. She later served as county recorder.

She had gone to the home of her daughter in North College Hill on Sunday, September 3, for a week's visit and on the day of her death had spent most of the day sewing. About

4:30 o'clock in the afternoon she had complained of a pain in her head and her condition grew steadily worse until she died about 8 o'clock that evening.

The body was removed to her home on West High Street Sunday afternoon and remained there until time for the funeral services on Monday. [69]

Mayme died a day before her birthday. She died months before James Anderson's parole hearing was decided. The burden of the wait is now Stella's.

The Governor's executive order is read on January 5, 1945. Had Mayme lived the order would have been anointed with her tears. Her illness and death were diagnosed as heart problems. Heart problems, indeed! A broken heart beset with the disappointment of justice not complete. She would now join Herman. James Anderson was alive and free after fourteen years, six months, and twenty-six days imprisoned. Stella is the only one left to read the words of the governor's order.

WHEREAS, One JAMES ANDERSON was convicted in the Circuit Court of Franklin County, Indiana on July 7, 1930 charged with First Degree Murder and sentenced and committed to the Indiana State Prison to Death; and

WHEREAS, His death sentence was afterwards commuted to a Life term; And WHEREAS, The trial prosecutor recommends granting clemency based on conduct of Anderson;

WHEREAS, Anderson has a good record and is recommended by institution authorities;

NOW THEREFORE, I, Henry F. Schricker, Governor of the State of Indiana, by virtue of the power and authority vested in me by the Constitution and laws of said State hereby

---

[69] *The Lawrenceburg Register,* 14 September 1945, 1

commute the Life sentence of the said James Anderson to a term of time served to Life.

WHEREAS, No prisoner is placed on parole merely as reward for good conduct or efficient performance of duties assigned in prison. Parole does not eliminate crime or forgive the offender.[70]

Parole is not an act of clemency, but a penological measure for the disciplinary treatment of prisoners capable of rehabilitation outside of prison walls. It does not set aside the sentence.[71]

Parole is not freedom. A parolee is a convicted criminal who has been sentenced to a term of imprisonment and who has been allowed to serve a portion of that term outside prison walls.[72]

A parolee does not enjoy liberty which every citizen is entitled, only a conditional liberty properly dependent on the observance of parole restrictions. By statute, a parolee is in legal custody. While on parole the convict is bound to remain in legal custody and under control of the warden until the expiration of the term...A parolee is not afforded the full constitutional protection enjoyed by ordinary citizens possessed of bull civil rights, and a search of a parolee's premises is not the be tested.[73]

As Governor Schricker commutes the Life sentence of James Anderson to time served, it is difficult for Stella to understand parole and its effects. Parole appears to be a "free pass" for the prisoner while the victim's family remains locked

---

[70] *Sellers v. Bridges,* 153 Fla. 586 (Fla. 1943)
[71] *Commonwealth ex. Rel. Banks v Cain,* 345 Pa. 581 (Pa. 1942)
[72] *United States v. Polito,* 583 F.2d 48 (2d Cir. N.Y. 1978)
[73] *State v. Williams,* 486 S. W. 2d 468 (Mo. 1972)

in the shackles of worry and wait. It is very difficult to understand and accept the legal effects of parole.

~

Dad's gone. Mom's gone. Anderson's free. If I don't think about it, I won't be bothered. The girls keep me busy. Margie and Martha start school. They look so nice in their bright school dresses. Mom and Dad would have been so pleased to watch them grow.

I'm pregnant again. Elaine grows bigger. Hopefully I'll be able to handle a young one without Elaine under foot full time. October 1, 1947 brings us a much hoped for blessing, a boy. Tommy has bright blue eyes, white blond hair, and a dimpled smile. He fills a great void left by Dad and Mom's departure.

The girls are in school and Tommy's walking. He's a handful. There's a man with a pony in the neighborhood. He's taking pictures of children on the pony. It will be wonderful—a remembrance of days on our Wrights Corner farm. I always treasure those days.

34

"Is the Well Dry?"

"A lawyer called me today. He says James Anderson is up for release. I can't believe it. He wants to talk about the coming Parole Board hearing."

Stella Mae Lange Fahey – *My Journal, 10/01/1950*

Our quiet life is being disrupted again. I receive a phone call from a lawyer. He wishes to speak to me about an upcoming hearing concerning James Anderson. I drop the phone. I want to hang up, but I listen to what he says. He wants me to meet with him at his Carew Tower office. Bill doesn't want me to go. Someone from the Dearborn County prosecutor's office calls to say that I must meet with this lawyer if there is to be any hope of keeping Anderson from being pardoned. They tell me I am the only living relative who can speak to the Parole Board against pardon of Dad's killer. I feel that the well of my emotions has run dry.

I already sent the girls off to school. A warm, late summer breeze stirs the air at the bus stop. The number seventeen bus to downtown Cincinnati screeches to a noisy stop. I switch Tommy to my left arm, freeing my right hand to toss two tokens into the driver's fare box. My stomach queases. Tommy squirms. I play in my head what I want to say to the lawyer. 'I'm scared, and I don't want that man to get me.'

My eye catches the street sign Fifth and Race. I pull the cord and I cradle Tommy back into my arm, heading out the rear door of the bus. I've been in some of the shops of the Carew Tower, but I have never been up into any of the offices in the upper floors. I recheck the letter in my hand and ask the elevator operator to take us to the sixteenth floor.

I find the lawyer's office. His secretary opens the door to his office and ushers us in. I sit with Tommy in my lap. He enters. He is older than I expected. His white hair touches the back of his shirt. His glasses sit at the edge of his nose, his eyes staring over the top of the rims. He reminds me of the suited, official looking men filling the Franklin County Courthouse. He pats Tommy's head, then asks me if I remember him. I don't.

"My name is Charles Baker." He smiles and continues, "I was one of the members of the Franklin County Prosecutor's team who helped your Judge Lowe present the case for the state in the death of your Father. I recall watching you sit so quiet and still through that entire trial. It must have been terrible for you."

"It was. I'm sorry, but I don't remember you. I don't remember much of the happenings of those days. The years have piled up like cordwood, indistinguishable from each other"

"I understand. I have been practicing law here in Ohio for a number of years now. I was recently notified of the Parole Board's query into the possible pardon of James Anderson. There are not many of us left from that trial, so I gladly offered to represent Herman's Family in the meeting with the Parole Board."

"I am so happy you are doing that. I was so afraid there was no one else left to stand up for Dad."

"Good. Let me take your deposition so that I can accurately portray your feelings before the board."

"Thank you."

~

Stella unloaded her feelings without the distress accompanying an audience with the Parole Board. Once again the Board looks to the family, friends, and participants in *State of Indiana vs. James Anderson* to decide Anderson's removal from parole. The ranks of those to testify are depleted. Ora Slater dead. Mayme gone. Attorney Baker represents Stella before the Parole Board swaying them to deny total freedom of a pardon to Anderson.

~

I am glad this is done. How long can I continue to bury the pain of the loss of Dad and Mom?

35

"Spells"

I went to see Doctor Wilke today. He doesn't know what's wrong with me.

Stella Mae Lange Fahey – *My Journal, 10/05/1959*

In the early fall of 1959 possibility of removal from parole arises again for Anderson. He may be pardoned. It's thirty years since the disturbance at "Spike's" bootleg camp along the Whitewater River led to Dad's murder and James Anderson's sentence of Death for First Degree Murder. A lot of water has flowed down the Whitewater River in those years. Torrents of heartache and tears flow since.

~

The Parole Board is certain to call upon Stella and any remaining trial participants once again for help in determination of Anderson's pardon. Time takes its toll. There are now even fewer first hand prosecution and judicial trial participants. More participants are dead. The passage of time clouds and erases some participant's memories. There is not the clarity of thought, the steadfastness of purpose, or the zeal for justice that was overflowing in 1930 and still brimming to the edge in 1945. Most all are beat down.

There are conditions to James Anderson's release from the restrictions of parole. He can commit no crime. He must successfully reintegrate into the community. He can only live in certain areas with Burlington, Kentucky being assigned to him by the Parole Board. He has to appear regularly before his Parole Officer to verify he meets all conditions. Will he meet these conditions? Will he be released from all restrictions impeding his living a free and unfettered life? He might. But Stella may not be released from her shackles of pain, loss, and fear.

I don't know if Stella ever met with the parole board. She is having some medical issues that drive her tale even deeper inside her. The years have beaten the memories from her mind like a hammer buries its nail into the wood.

~

I went to see that lawyer years ago to convince the parole board not to agree to a pardon for Anderson. I don't want to go again. I don't know what to do.

I feel dizzy. I'm light-headed. My mind fails me. My thoughts assail me. I want to be done with all this. I can't think about this.

Pop…pop., then pop…pop…pop…pop…pop…pop. Two thoughts, then six thoughts burst again and again. Or, is it two shots fatal, then six shots futile. Just like the newspapers said it happened. Dad died. Anderson lived.

I must stop.

~

I am Stella's son. I'm afraid I must take up her story at this point. I am eleven in the early fall of 1959. I have no recall of James Anderson, his release from restrictions of parole, my mother's angst over the potential total freedom for her father's murderer. I do have a very vivid recollection of something very frightening I encountered that October day.

~

Returning home from school I open our side door and launch myself up the four steps leading to the kitchen. There by the counter stands Mom. I yell "Hi" at her; and before I can turn and run up the stairs to my room, I notice something very unusual. Mom does not greet me. She stands stiff as a board with one hand leaning against the counter. She stares blindly into space, her eyes looking right through me. Her lip makes a strange twitch. I bawl, "What's wrong?" She is silent and continues to look past me. Her grip on the counter loosens, her eyes roll into her head, and she falls to the floor like a load of wet laundry.

Panic stricken, I bolt out of the house and bound to the neighbor's house screaming at the top of my lungs for Elsie. She grabs my hand and I drag her back to our kitchen as quickly as we both can travel. Entering the house, I can see that Mom is no longer flat on the floor but she is sitting on it. Elsie grabs Mom under the arm and helps her to a chair in the dining room. She begins to care for mom and tells me to go upstairs and change my clothes. She assures me that my mom will be all right.

After a while Elsie returns home. Mom begins to prepare dinner. She says nothing to me. She acts as if nothing has happened. Whatever demons grab her, whatever seizure she endures, whatever spell she falls under is never revealed to me. The rest of that day is a blur to me.

I never know and am never told what ails Mom. She has more of these spells or seizures through the rest of her life. Although I am nearby for many of these episodes, I never can determine some trigger that would set them off. Were they caused by iron deficiencies? Were they related to some stress? Were they a type of seizure or epilepsy? Her doctors never identify and certainly never cure the episodes.

I have my own diagnosis. I am no doctor, but I think I know what got them started. The spell I encounter in September, 1959, could be the first spell Mom endures. I believe the pain and the stress of reopening wounds caused by her father, Herman's murder brings her to her knees. As much as she tries to bury all the pain, fate keeps digging it back up. Manhunts, trials, retrial appeals, Supreme Court hearings, stays of execution, parole board recommendations, governor's clemency decisions each pick away at the scabs covering her wounds. Her spells are the infections of unhealing wounds.

James Anderson is discharged from parole. Governor's Executive Order Number 22180 signed by Harold Hanley releases him from all restrictions on January 11, 1960. James Anderson is pardoned. He is a free man.

WHEREAS, One James Anderson convicted in the Circuit Court of Franklin County, Indiana, on July 7, 1930, charged with First Degree Murder sentenced and committed to the Indiana State Prison to Death;

WHEREAS, On December 7, 1933 the Death Sentence of the said Anderson was commuted to a term of Life; and

WHEREAS, On January 5, 1945, under authority of Executive Order #17970 his Life Sentence was commuted to a term of 14 years, 6 months and 28 days to Life and he was subsequently released on parole September 18, 1945; and

WHEREAS ,It is made to appear that the said Anderson has conducted himself in an exemplary manner since the date of his parole and the Division of Parole recommends that he be granted a discharge; and

WHEREAS, The Board of Correction, after a careful investigation and examination of all the facts in the case, recommends that the said Anderson be granted a discharge from parole by commutation of sentence;

THEREFORE, I, Harold W. Handley, Governor of the State of Indiana, by virtue of the power and authority vested in me by the Constitution and laws of said State, hereby commute the Life Sentence of the said James Anderson to a term of Time Served.

TESTIMONY WEREOF, I have hereunto set my hand and caused to be affixed the Great Seal of the State of Indiana, at the Capital, in the City of Indianapolis, this 11th day of January, 1960.

Harold W. Handley[74]

       Stella always feared retaliation and revenge. There was probably no real menace, but she always felt there was. James Anderson went to work for the Big Four Railroad. He married and raised two children in Burlington, Kentucky. I'm sure Mom never knew how close he was. She didn't need to

---

[74] *Governor Harold W. Handley, State of Indiana, Executive Order #22180, 20 January 1960*

know. The demons were there for her anyway.

This one small, stained, worn piece of paper traces a litany of dates, each one of which dug at Mom's heart.

Anderson Prison Record Documenting Clemency and Parole

36

"We are There!"

We went to visit the Fahey's yesterday in Aurora. We stopped at Greendale Cemetery first. Tommy asked me why we stopped there. That's a tough question. Every time we visit Dad and Mom's grave site, I remember why I miss them so much. They were everything to me and I loved them dearly. When he gets older I'll share my stories of Herman and Mayme with Tommy.

Stella Mae Lange Fahey – *My Journal, 09/09/1953*

It's September, 1953. I was six years old. This is where I began the quest, "Are we there yet?" It's now January, 2020. Over sixty-five years have passed. Stella never revealed her stories to me. I've learned a lot. I've uncovered much. I never met them, but I now feel I know Herman and Mayme. They are unseen grandparents, but not unknown.

Digging out the story, I now know Herman and Mayme loved each other. They loved their daughter, Stella. They loved the land, all seventy-one acres of it. They were determined to survive. They would make it as farmers or they would make it as elected law enforcement; but they would make it.

Their morals were nurtured by strong family and solid

religious background. They had an unwavering sense of duty. They had a duty to improve their political party. They had a duty to serve their county and its people. They had a duty to respect and forever remember those who helped them along the way.

They surrounded themselves with good people, or sometimes good people just happened to surround them. They were unrelenting in their desire to do what was right. Yes, I have learned to know my grandparents.

My memory of Herman and Mayme began for me as a source of my childish annoyance on a drive from Cincinnati to Aurora. They were just names on a tombstone in Greendale Cemetery. They became much more. The dashes on their tombstone between birth date and death date overflowed with the meaningfulness of their lives. My youthful question is answered. "We are there!"

Herman and Mayme are now more than I had ever dreamed. They went from being nothing in my mind to something much bigger than I could ever imagine. I regret that I did not know them at my age of six as I know them today.

In 2009 I met Dave Lusby, then Sheriff of Dearborn County. With my research and Dave's desire and connections, Herman Lange and his story moved from the microfilm pages in the Lawrenceburg and Indiana State Libraries to the limestone wall at the National Law Enforcement Officers Memorial on Judiciary Square in Washington, D.C.

Each year names of law enforcement agents who have fallen in the line of duty in the previous year or who have fallen in prior years and not yet added are carved onto the limestone walls at the National Memorial. Each year on May 13 those officers whose names have been added to the walls are honored at a candlelight vigil in the nation's capital. Dave cut through the red tape to get Herman's name added to the memorial and have his story heard.

Law Enforcement Officers Memorial, Washington, D.C.

The mission of the National Law Enforcement Officers Memorial is to generate increased public support for the law enforcement profession by permanently recording and appropriately commemorating the service and sacrifice of law enforcement officers; and to provide information that will help promote law enforcement safety.

Seven years after passage of the authorizing legislation, on October 15, 1991, the Memorial was officially dedicated. At the time of dedication, the names of over 12,000 fallen officers were engraved on the Memorial's walls. Currently, there are 19,660 names on the Memorial. Each year, during National Police Week, on May 13, there is a Candlelight Vigil, attended by more than 20,000 officers and survivors, to formally dedicate the names added to the Memorial walls that year. In 2010, 323 total names were added to the Walls, 120 were fallen officers from 2009 and 203 were line-of-duty deaths that occurred earlier in U.S. history but had just recently come to light. One of those historic additions made in the 2010 ceremony was the name of Herman Thomas Lange, fallen Sheriff of Dearborn County, Indiana

The Board of Directors & Staff
of the
National Law Enforcement Officers Memorial Fund
request the honor of your presence
at the

22nd Annual Candlelight Vigil

on Thursday the thirteenth of May
two thousand and ten
at eight o'clock in the evening
on the grounds of the

National Law Enforcement Officers Memorial
Judiciary Square
Washington, District of Columbia

The reading of the
Roll Call of Fallen Heroes
to immediately follow

Metro Red Line
Judiciary Square Station

Invitation to 2010 Candlelight Vigil Washington, D.C.
The walls, upon which honored officers' names are carved, flow around the tree lined grounds of the Memorial.

The Memorial features four bronze lions, two male and two female, each watching over a pair of lion cubs. The adult lions were sculpted by Raymond Katsey, the cubs by George Carr. Below each lion is carved a different quotation.

Bronze Lion on Path of Memorial for Fallen Police Officers

"It is not how these officers died that made them heroes, it is how they lived." Vivian Eney Cross, Survivor.

"In valor there is hope." Tacitus.

"The wicked flee when no man pursueth: but the righteous are bold as a lion." Proverbs 28:1. "Carved on these walls is the story of America, of a continuing quest to preserve both democracy and decency, and to protect a national treasure that we call the American dream." President George H. W. Bush

With the help of members of Indiana C.O.P.S. (Concerns of Police Survivors), my wife and I and two of our children traveled to Washington to attend Herman's induction at the May 13, 2010 candlelight vigil. I never knew Herman but his addition to the memorial molded all the hundreds of feet of microfilm into a flesh and blood man for whom I was overcome with pride. I found Herman's name carved onto the limestone wall and I cried. I heard Herman's name and "End of Watch" announcement at the vigil and I cried. Those tears poured out of my heart and into my memory to wash away all the years of not knowing the man, Herman Lange.

It was truly a humbling and emotional experience sitting among the hundreds of friends, relatives, and fellow officers whose loved ones were being honored. Just as these people tearfully remembered and grieved the departed fallen, so too must Mayme and Stella have remembered Herman. The Lange women grieved not at the limestone and marble monuments of Washington, but at the simple headstone in Greendale Cemetery.

Me and Wife Kathy at Memorial Wall, Washington D.C.

There is to be one more memorial to Herman Lange later in 2010. In Indianapolis in late September at the Indiana Law Enforcement and Fire Fighters Memorial, Herman's name is to be engraved onto the memorial's "Roll Call of Fallen Heroes."

At the Indianapolis memorial service, there is time to

recognize each of the fallen officers. Herman gets his due time. The speaker's words tell all present of Herman's devotion to the duty of serving his County even at the price of his own life. There are more than names carved in recognition on limestone walls. There are now the words of Herman's story to flesh out his life. The speaker's words ring out. The story on the various fallen heroes' websites rings out.

The honor of your presence is requested on Wednesday, September 29, 2010, for the Indiana Fraternal Order of Police Memorial Service.

Please join us as we honor the officers who have died in the line of duty, their families, the departments they served, and the sacrifice they have made.

Memorial Service: 2:00 P.M. Indiana Law Enforcement and Fire Fighters Memorial Indianapolis, Indiana

Indiana Law Enforcement and Fire Fighters Memorial is located behind the West side of the Indiana State Capitol, at the corner of Government Way and Senate Avenue in Indianapolis, IN

In case of inclement weather, the ceremony will be held in the Capitol Rotunda.

Invitation to Service Indiana Law Enforcement Memorial

One more piece falls into place at the Indianapolis memorial. As the story of Herman is told, there is a chapter added. Mayme is recognized not only as an Indiana County Sheriff completing her husband's term of duty, but she is also recognized as being the 'first' woman sheriff in Dearborn

County and in the State of Indiana. Both now are being recognized for what they are, important servants of their Dearborn County.

When I was age six, the limestone monuments in Greendale above the graves of Herman and Mayme held no meaning for me. I had no understanding of the effect the carved tombstones had on my mother. The tombstones reminded her of grief for parents lost and hope extinguished.

Indiana Memorial Bearing Herman's Name

The carved limestone in Washington D. C. and Indianapolis, Indiana holds a lot of meaning for me. The etchings on the monuments affect me dramatically. They offer me pride and gratitude for grandparents so real and notable. I wish my mother could see Herman and Mayme honored. These walls would bring her pride in parents remembered.

I still may not have the entire story. I am satisfied that I have enough of the story to affirm the importance of Herman and Mayme for me. I believe there is enough in the story for all of my family to take pride in the special lives of their ancestors. The unlocked story is a good one.

Stella's grief over the tragic loss of her Father was overpowering for her fifteen year-old self. Grief is not neat and orderly; it does not follow any rules. Time does not heal it. Rather, time insists on passing, and as it does, grief changes but does not go away. Grief is not a wave that came unexpectedly and swept Stella away. It was a wall of pain that grabbed hold and battered Stella day after day. Some days, Stella could take some comfort in grief's lesser tap, tap, tap on her shoulder. Some days, still, after all this time, Stella would be consumed by grief and she wondered if there was any way free of it.

More than anything I wish that this story would have been told by Stella. She died in 2002. I pray that she finds the shade of a tree on a heavenly knoll from which she can page through this book and know that she is loved by me and Herman and Mayme. Be proud, Mom. You were part of a great story. No more tears. No more fears. No more grief. The key to your locked story is here now. I hope I have helped you unlock it. I will grab that key your imagined words offered me. I will share your story with everyone who will listen. Your time of mourning is over. Our, your story-telling time is now.

It is suffering, death, loss, grief, struggle, fear that is locked away. Unlock and those sorrowful memories fly away. What you really find is love, honor, duty, dedication, hard work.

Thomas Fahey